Urban Multiculturalism and Globalization in
New York City

Urban Multiculturalism and Globalization in New York City

An Analysis of Diasporic Temporalities

Michel S. Laguerre
University of California at Berkeley

First published 2003 by
PALGRAVE MACMILLAN
Houndmills, Basingstoke, Hampshire RG21 6XS and 175 Fifth Avenue, New York, N.Y. 10010
Companies and representatives throughout the world

PALGRAVE MACMILLAN is the global academic imprint of the Palgrave Macmillan division of St. Martin's Press, LLC and of Palgrave Macmillan Ltd. Macmillan® is a registered trademark in the United States, United Kingdom and other countries. Palgrave is a registered trademark in the European Union and other countries.

ISBN 1403915512 hardback

This book is printed on paper suitable for recycling and made from fully managed and sustained forest sources.

A catalogue record for this book is available from the British Library.

Library of Congress Cataloging-in-Publication Data

Laguerre, Michel S.
    Urban multiculturalism and globalization in New York City :
an analysis of diasporic temporalities / Michel S. Laguerre.
        p.   cm.
    Includes bibliographical references and index.
    ISBN 1–4039–1551–2 (cloth)
    1. New York (N.Y.)–Social conditions.   2. Immigrants–New
York (State)–New York.   3. Multiculturalism–New York (State)–
New York.   4. Globalization–Social aspects–New York (State)–
New York.   5. San Francisco Bay Area (Calif.)–Social conditions.
    6. Immigrants–San Francisco Bay Area.
    7. Multiculturalism–California–San Francisco Bay Area.
    8. Globalization–Social aspects–California–San Francisco Bay Area.
    I. Title.

HN80.N5L34   2003
306'.09747'1–dc21

                                                      2003051439

10   9   8   7   6   5   4   3   2   1
12   11   10   09   08   07   06   05   04   03

Printed and bound in Great Britain by
Antony Rowe Ltd, Chippenham and Eastbourne

In memory of the victims of 9/11.
Requiescant in pacem!

Contents

List of Tables

Acknowledgments

The preparation of this book has benefited from the help of various institutions and individuals. The Berkeley Center for Globalization and Information Technology, the Jewish Theological Seminary (New York), The Graduate Theological Union (Berkeley), the Institute of Governmental Studies Library, the Boalt Law School Library and Doe Library at the University of California at Berkeley, the Islamic Center and the Islamic Mosque (Manhattan), the Northern California Islamic Center (Oakland), Jewish merchants in the Diamond District of Manhattan, and several Muslims, Jews, and others with whom I have had an opportunity to discuss their views and practices of diasporic time.

The project was blessed to enlist the cooperation of a few Berkeley students from the Undergraduate Research Apprenticeship Program who helped with bibliographical searches in various databases, transcriptions of texts, and discussing with me the orientation of the project. I want to thank them for having been such dedicated researchers: Gee Wah Mok, Peter Chung, Linda Peng, Ann Thuy Le, Stephanie Sadre-Orafai, Laleh Shahabi, Smitri Rana, Jacob Averbuck, Brooke Ashe, Julia Zamorisca, Sara Abramowitz-Hill, Carol Chu, Jennifer Yee, Ann Pu, and Sara Razavi. I also wish to thank the students who took my American Studies seminar on "The Week" for some productive discussions. I am furthermore grateful to Kathy Gough and three anonymous reviewers for their critical comments, to Deana Abramowitz and Hatem Bazian for their keen observations pertaining to aspects discussed in this book, and to Bud Bynack, who copyedited with great care and professionalism the final draft of the book. Last, but not least, I owe considerable thanks to my editors at Palgrave Macmillan Limited, especially Heather Gibson, Jennifer Nelson, and Briar Towers, and to Bruce Cain, Terry Dean, and Marc Levin at the Institute of Governmental Studies.

Portions of the book were delivered in various academic forums, including the Department of Geography at Louisiana State University, Baton Rouge; the Department of Sociology and Anthropology at Colgate University; the Program in Religious Studies at the University of California, Davis; the annual meetings of the American Sociological Association (Urban Sociology and International Migration sections); and the International Symposium on Diaspora and Homeland organized by the Armenian and Post-Soviet Studies at the University of California, Berkeley.

Finally I am thankful to Ellie Perelman for the index and Linda Auld for overseeing the production of the book.

Introduction

On September 11, 2001, New York City residents awoke to witness unexpectedly the forceful deployment of a horrific and devastating event that was going to affect every aspect of social life. Two attacks on the World Trade Center, masterminded and carried out with some precision by Muslim extremists, not only destroyed the two architecturally elegant towers that for many years graced the skies of Manhattan and served as a global financial transactional center, but also caused the death of countless innocent victims of diverse faiths and ethnic backgrounds. The anti-Muslim sentiment that these deadly hijacked jetliner attacks suddenly stirred up from among the larger population gives us cause to revisit the multiethnic, multireligious makeup of the city and to view it from a new angle – that of its multitemporal character.

New York is a quintessential diasporic city because of the numerous immigrant groups that have forged distinct cultural niches in its midst. They have come to the city at different periods of its history, sometimes directly from abroad, and at other times as a result of secondary migrations, as, for example, in the case of the huge Afro-American population from the southern region of the United States that fed the neighborhoods of Harlem and Brooklyn in the first quarter of the twentieth century.

While some of these immigrants have long adopted the Western mode of time reckoning as a pivot of their socialization, others, who grew up under a different temporal regime, find it necessary to negotiate their temporal insertion in the city more gradually. Time thus is an important dimension around which the articulation of diasporic communities can be analyzed, deciphered, and understood.

1

While diasporic practices of temporality in New York display singular peculiarities because of their global modes of operation, the phenomenon is not exclusive to any locale or immigrant group, but is universal in its manifestation. In cities throughout the globe, from Paris, Beijing, or Jerusalem to Cairo, New Delhi, or Port-au-Prince, diasporic communities have maintained a temporal rhythm of life different from that of the mainstream. In the West, they carve out niches for their distinct temporalities in the midst of the hegemonic temporal regime. In these temporal enclaves, they follow their national calendars of ethnic holy days and holidays, separate from, and in competition with, mainstream practices. This is a global phenomenon that occurs in immigrant communities because, while they seek out economic and political integration, they are less eager to give up the traditional practices of temporality that cadence the religious and national symbols of their life.

This book explains how the existence and use of ethnic temporality distinguishes the cultural ways of some immigrant communities from the mainstream, why such a diasporic practice, because it is encrusted in religious and national ideologies, will not vanish, despite acculturation in other spheres of life, and how these different temporal practices fracture the temporal matrix of the city while at the same time accounting for the subaltern integration of some immigrant enclaves.

For many years, the study of diasporic communities has been done from the standpoint of space because of the visibility that their geographic concentration affords and because of the prevalent practice of housing segregation. State intervention, once the diagnosis is made, is often sought to alleviate the burden. This has fueled a policy debate on racial discrimination among mainstreamers to find a solution to what is considered to be a shortcoming in the practice of democracy. Strangely enough, a similar level of awareness pertaining to ethnic temporality is yet to be achieved by the larger population. In other words, temporal ghettoization has not attracted the same kind of debate as has spatial ghettoization. In contrast, minoritized groups whose calendars have been subalternized see temporal subjugation as a form of discrimination that is both financially costly for their communities and a burden as they are called upon to negotiate between two temporalities and to uphold the requirements of both.

This book explains the ramifications of temporal ghettoization for immigrants and the larger society. It not only spells out the logic behind ethnic calendars and explains how they operate, but it also examines the behavioral ramifications of the incorporation of these temporal systems into the everyday life of New Yorkers. What emerges from our analysis is a recognition not only of the existence of separate temporal systems, but also of the multiplicity of times that are bodily integrated and behaviorally expressed as individuals move from one calendar to the other to accomplish specific ends or for specific purposes. While these temporal systems continue to have their own separate identities, some immigrants appropriate them at different times for different reasons.

The study of the temporal dimension of diasporic communities sheds light on transglobal diasporic integration because it shows how time fractures the trajectories of subjectivity, identity, ethnicity, inequality, and space. Multiculturalism has a temporal dimension, and so does inequality. The city of New York provides us a way to examine the temporal order of things, or more precisely, how time intervenes in the architecture of power relations between hegemony and subalternity.

In an effort to explain the importance of diasporic temporalities as a factor in the integration of immigrants in the American metropolis, Chapter 1 introduces the concept of the "chronopolis" by way of unveiling and analytically dissecting the plurality of diasporic temporalities in New York City. After a sustained, but brief review of the literature on the sociology of time, it defines a chronopolis as an urban enclave – distinguished by a temporal orientation different from that of the mainstream – that articulates itself with the larger urban system through the mechanism of its subalternized temporal logic. It proposes that a focus on subalternized time is likely to shed a great deal of light on the social organization of the American city because it is a multidimensional site for the inscription of diasporic enclaves and of their interface with the mainstream community. It further argues that the city is traversed by temporal flows that are transnational and transglobal in nature and that intrinsically shape local community life and influence in various ways the mainstream urban system. It explains how diasporic temporalities fragment the social landscape of the city, link its components to overseas sites, globalize that relationship through the deployment of transnational networks, and, in the process, give rise to localized global chronopolises. Ultimately, it shows how the transglobalization of the city accounts for the existence of its multiple temporal identities.

Although the civil week is hegemonic because it regulates affairs of state and provides a mechanism for social order, it should not be confused with the Christian week. Chapter 2 distinguishes these two temporal orders, identifies the social identity of both the civil week and the Christian week, and shows how they have evolved differently because of their distinct rationales. It does so by comparing the peak day of the civil week with those of the Jewish, Christian, and Muslim weekly cycles. It contrasts the civil Sunday with the Christian Sunday through an examination of New York's "blue laws." It explains how the blue laws provide a frame of reference for the policing and criminalization of Sunday activities unrelated to churchgoing and how they have been used to subalternize and discipline the other weekly cycles. Since racial practices have a temporal infrastructure, the chapter also seeks to explain the race of the civil week, or how race implodes inside of hegemonic time. The civil week is shown to be not only a local production, but also the outcome of a global process.

Chapter 3 investigates specific aspects of Jewish temporality in New York City. It delineates the genealogy of the subalternity of Jewish temporality and shows how temporal rights gained in one institution (for example, the military) were used to acquire similar rights in other areas of social life (the labor market and the school system). It shows the importance of "the day of preparation" in the Jewish weekly cycle and how the location of the Sabbath on the seventh day affects diasporic business. It identifies two mechanisms used by Jewish New Yorkers to deal with the idiosyncrasies of their cultural temporal practices, namely, a strategy of temporal substitution and a strategy of spatial–temporal expansion through the reordering of the landscape. It further explains how the globalization of these temporal practices has been a main engine in the transformation of the identity politics of Jewish New Yorkers.

Muslim immigrant enclaves in New York City provide an exemplary pan-Islamic site for the operationalization and application of the concept of the chronopolis precisely because of the multiple ethnicities of these diasporic groups. Chapter 4 explains how the Muslim week has adapted to the constraints of the civil week and how Muslims negotiate in the workplace for religious tolerance so that they may perform their daily prayerful rituals. Here we examine how the temporal disjuncture between the hegemonic civil week and the subalternized Muslim week has produced two different temporal cycles that crisscross each other without each losing its distinct identity. The chapter shows how, irrespective of the national origin of the immigrants, this diasporic weekly cycle provides a temporal infrastructure to secular and religious activities that it is pivotal for us to grasp in order to understand the integration of this global chronopolis in the social structure of the city.

Chapter 5 proposes that diasporic new years, holy days, and holidays incubate the memory of the homeland, heighten the temporal dissimilarity between the mainstream and the ethnic enclave, intensify transnational relations, maximize revenues in the diasporic economy, slow down aspects of the mainstream economy because of the ephemeral absence of these actors in the labor market, raise the public consciousness about the presence of the group in their midst, induce changes in the ways of the mainstream to accommodate the needs of the diasporic community, and help the group reproduce itself as a transglobal entity. The chapter explains how immigrants have used these subaltern holidays to ensure the reproduction of their transnational communities. It further shows how these holidays alter the scheduling of classes in the New York City public school system and the alternate-side-of-the-street street-sweeping programs of the municipal government, thereby affecting not only the diasporans, but also the larger urban community.

Finally the Conclusion relocates my critical reflections on diasporic temporalities inside the literature on transnationalization and globalization. It indicates that the diasporic weekly cycles that coexist in New York City provide a multilayered temporal basis from which the dynamics of urban multiculturalism can be understood. It further shows how the global aspects of multiculturalism are an intrinsic engine that help shape its local articulation and are a contributing factor to the global identity not only of the chronopolis, but also of the global city.

1
Transglobality and Diasporic Temporality

This book focuses on American society as a transglobal nation and examines the temporal dimension of diasporic incorporation in New York City and the San Francisco Bay Area. It argues that immigrant neighborhoods are faced not only with issues of economic and political integration, but also are engaged in a sublime and relentless effort of harmonizing the cultural rhythms of their daily life with the hegemonic temporality of mainstream society. Although much energy has been spent in explaining the segregated or ghettoized space of ethnic communities,[1] there is, in contrast, a dearth of data on the subalternization, genealogy, and inscription of minoritized temporalities in the structural and interactional organization of the multicultural American city.[2]

Time, of course, is taken into consideration in emphasizing phases of immigration, the history of the incorporation of immigrants in American society, the adaptation of immigrants to industrial time, and the differing length of time it took for different groups to assimilate with the mainstream culture. That, however, is not what concerns us here. How ludicrous could it be to believe that it is unnecessary to forego the immigrant's sense of time and to assume that the blending with the mainstream time will be a smooth transaction and transition? In fact, temporal adjustment may remain part of a continuous process of adaptation. It is so precisely because diasporic temporalities are sustained by religious and cultural differentiation, by the cultures in which immigrants are imbedded. The time of the diasporic religion or diasporic culture informs not only the first, but also subsequent generations. Just as Jews have been in the West for at least two millennia, but the institution of the Sabbath has remained central to the daily life of some, and the Jewish calendar, however diasporized, remains a principal marker for their time reckoning, so it is with other groups, other temporalities.

The multiple temporal identities of the city

Identity is often theorized in terms of culture, ethnicity, gender, and space, but seldom in terms of time. However, identity has a temporal frame of reference. Diasporic enclaves display multiple temporal identities, as well as identities based on race, ethnicity, or other factors – identities that contribute to the complex dynamics of the city. New York City is a multidiasporic urban landscape, each ethnic enclave attaining to the preservation of its cultural heritage while at the same time being shaped by and contributing to the mainstream.

Diasporic communities differ in the way they use their temporalities to express their cultural authenticity for themselves and for public consumption by the mainstream. It is sometimes done via a public display, as in the case of the Chinese New Year. In other cases, it involves only members of the group, as in the case of Jewish High Holidays and the Muslim observance of Ramadan. Unlike the public events, which attract the interaction of members of the mainstream with the diasporic community, these tend to isolate the community from the rest of the city.

The American city contains many different diasporic temporalities. These are hierarchized depending on the status of the group in society. Instead of the prevalent dual structure of hegemony and subalternity, now one witnesses a multiplicity of subaltern temporalities next to each other in the same space. This book examines their interaction with the hegemonic temporality of Western time.

In its principal focus, the book studies the mode of articulation of the three religion-based weeks inside the hegemonic civil week. It investigates the adaptation of the Islamic week, which peaks on Friday (the day of the mandatory congregational prayer), the Jewish week, which culminates with the observance of the Sabbath on Saturday, and the Christian week, which recognizes Sunday as a day of worship. It also analyzes the hegemonic status of the civil week and how it disciplines the behaviors of the other weekly cycles through the creative mechanism of the "blue laws"[3] or "Sunday legislation" as enacted and implemented in New York City.

The book also investigates the relation of subaltern temporalities to the temporalities of the hegemonic mainstream via an examination of diasporic new years and subalternized holidays (including holy days) that are celebrated in immigrant communities in New York City and San Francisco and that do not coincide with mainstream society's New Year's Day and national and state holidays. It examines the participation of diasporic citizens in the hegemonic (January 1) New Year and in ethnic New Year festivities as diverse as the Chinese New Year in late January or early February, the Iranian New Year on March 21, and the Jewish New Year in mid-September or early October, along with other diasporic holidays such as the Jewish High Holidays and shows their differential impact on social life in San Francisco and New York City.

This book demonstrates that the American city is traversed by diverse transnational temporal flows that crisscross, but do not coincide with the mainstream temporal itinerary or trajectory. Further, it argues that these temporal flows are by nature global, since they are an extension of homeland cultural practices and as such are diasporized, transglobalized, and operative precisely because they are sustained by ongoing transnational relations.

It thus provides a different perspective on the relations between "the West" and "the Rest," as the distinction sometimes is drawn. Although prior to Columbus's voyage to the new world there were widespread population movements with the Muslim conquests in Europe, Africa, and Asia, and intra-European, American, and African migrations, it was only in the fifteenth century that the West made its systematic penetration of the Rest.[4] This penetration via colonization and slavery led to an incremental Westernization of the Rest. Chief among this Westernization process was the imposition of Western time, which implies standardization and affects the organization of the week, the structuring of the month, and the deployment of the year.[5]

What concerns us here, however, is not the Westernization of the Rest. We recognize instead that colonization was not always complete and failed to erase national calendars that regulate the religious and cultural life of the natives. Only total conversion to Christianity would have made that temporal conversion possible. Cultural resiliency has allowed the calendars of the natives to survive, despite constant assaults by the West and the dominant or hegemonic position of the Gregorian calendar.[6]

In addition to the insertion of Western temporality into the lives of the Rest, in short, there has been an insertion of the temporalities of the Rest in the lives of the West. For centuries, both as immigrants and at home, the Rest have resisted the imposition of Western time and have brought ways of preserving non-Western temporalities with them as immigrants. Granted that in some places, as in the case in the Anglophone countries of the Caribbean (Barbados, for example), Western temporal sequences simply have been accepted via assimilation, in others, adaptation and resistance have gone hand in hand, as in the case of the official coexistence of two systems of temporality, the Gregorian and Islamic calendars, in Egypt. In still others, the native system has remained dominant, as in the hegemonic position maintained by the Jewish calendar in Israel and the Muslim calendar in Saudi Arabia.

This study deals with immigrants to the United States from non-Western countries where these two strategies of resistance have prevailed: countries that have formally adopted the Western Gregorian calendar, which is a sixteenth-century adaptation of the Julian calendar,[7] and countries that use their native calendar as the official calendar of the state. Immigrants from the first informally use their native calendar, as in the case of Muslim Turkey, which chose Sunday as the day of rest instead of Friday, the chosen day in other Muslim countries. Immigrants from the latter, particularly for those from Israel and earlier Jewish immigrants with strong ties with Israel, formally observe a calendar where the day of rest coincides with the day of worship, the Sabbath, or Saturday, and where Jewish holy days are celebrated as national holidays, in contrast to Christian holidays or feast days. Thus, for those concerned, immigration to an American city such as New York entails the passage from a "Friday" (Muslim) or "Saturday" (Jewish) legislative regime to a site under a "Sunday" legislative regime.[8]

This book concerns itself with how immigrants who came from these countries have adapted to Western temporalities that subalternize the temporal practices of their communities.[9] Whether these immigrants have come from a country where their native calendar plays a dominant or subordinate role, their presence in the American city calls for an examination of the interface and interaction of their calendars with that of the West.

In the study of the American week, two aspects of globality appear: universal globality versus particular or specific globality, and dominant globality versus subaltern globality.[10] Universal globality indicates that the structure of dominance implicit in the Western week influences, shapes, and structures the activities of the world as a whole in terms of work days, economic transactions, and international relations. Particular globality refers to the limited global scope and the subaltern nature of the non-Western week as it is insinuated through migration and international relations in the Christian-influenced Western week. This hybridized week of the Rest incorporated inside the hegemonic week of the West competes in its own way for dominance – for dominant globality. The strategies of the non-Western Westernized week reflect and are an adaptation to the structure of domination of the Western week. Further, the non-Western diasporic week is in harmony with the religious observance of the calendar of the homeland. It is thus a subaltern globality. The book also unveils and explains the global aspects of the hegemonic and subaltern weekly cycles as they unfold in the United States, the relations of these weeks to each other, and the adjustment of the subaltern weeks to the civil week.

The question of the origin of the three peak days that separate Jews from Christians and Muslims has been addressed before, and my focus will not be on delineating the historical sequence or genealogy of these three weekly cycles,[11] but rather on explaining how in the West, Jews and Muslims have adapted to the Western weekly rhythm, how they have maintained their weekly schedules, how these weeks intersect, advantages and disadvantages they garner from this arrangement, how the maintenance of the temporal structure of their diasporic week enhances their globalization, how the dominant week interferes with their religious practices, how the dominant system has coerced them to abandon their week cycle, how their week "rhythms" daily life in their enclaves and in urban America, and how nonbelievers among these diasporas are influenced by these different cycles.

Temporal disjuncture

The immigrant finds a mainstream temporal system that has its own history. Such a history has evolved under pressure from industrialization, new laws concerning work time, vacation time for workers, and religious regulations on days of worship and rest. The immigrant is inserted in the evolving time of the dominant sector. However, because of cultural differences, these two times never collapse into one and exist next to each other. In that vein, Bhabha[12] speaks of the "disjunctive temporalities of the national culture."

For many years, communities with different rhythms of life have lived in peaceful coexistence as they both participate in the civil week and during their peak days, ethnic holidays, or prayer times withdraw from the mainstream temporal rhythms to return to their own diasporic temporal cadence. Yet immigrants who originally were used to a different weekly cycle experience as diasporans what Hassard[13] refers to as a "change in time consciousness." They find that their temporal sequence becomes subjugated, and that they must adjust their temporality to that of the mainstream. This often goes with a period of soul searching whereby temporal aspects that are not essential fade away and those that constitute core elements of the culture remain. In this subjugated niche, the subaltern may experience difficulties when she moves from one cultural time to the other.[14]

Because of their cultural background, the time and form of their incorporation and their relations with the mainstream, these immigrant communities have developed diasporic temporalities that are not simple duplicates of the homeland's, but that also bear the imprint of their new land of adoption. To understand their level of integration, one must pay attention to the "differential temporalities of their cultural histories."[15] These temporalities have both a local content (adaptation to the milieu) and a global content (relations with the homeland or continuity of homeland practices).

One must pay attention to the immigrant's time because it informs the rhythm of socialization in the new country, the speed with which adaptation occurs, group conflicts between different perceptions of time, generational conflicts among immigrants between parents and children, diasporic holy days and holidays, and the recognition of different temporal perspectives within a given nation. Guha, in his poststructuralist reflections on migrant's time, captures well the intricacies of the problem as he provides a temporal perspective on issues faced by migrants in their new land of adaptation. He notes:

> This is why switching communities is in every instance the occasion of a temporal maladjustment which, however, is grasped by common sense, not for what it is, but as the failure of one culture to slot smoothly into another. There is nothing particularly wrong with this interpretation except that it makes a part stand in for the whole. For what is cultural about this phenomenon is already entailed in the temporal and follows directly from it.... As an immigrant ... the sense of time he brings with him is the child of another temporality.[16]

Immigrant groups, once socialized in the cultural time of the homeland and cognizant of their resocialization in the United States, develop hybrid temporal perspectives that reproduce themselves over time through the marking of weekly ethnic peak days and subaltern holidays. These temporalities become hybridized through their interaction with mainstream temporalities and because of mainstream constraints. The diasporic experience is fundamentally one of both time change and continuity.[17] This diasporic time, which is dominated by the mainstream cultural time, is constructed in a state of subordination. Diasporic time covers the reconstituted time of the immigrants, their interpretation of the mainstream or dominant time and interaction time, and the relations of ethnic time to the dominant time.

Once we recognize these different diasporic times, we become more aware of the various cultural temporalities of the nation. The mainstream temporality is simply one among many others. As Bhabha[18] notes, "the national culture comes to be articulated as a dialectic of various temporalities – modern, colonial, postcolonial, native." The diasporic is but one moment in a more complicated diasporic temporality that expands, globalizes, and adapts homeland temporality to an extraterritorial environment.

The plurality of diasporic times can be approached in many ways. The idea of "multiple time" or "multiple manifestations of time" put forward by the French sociologist Georges Gurvitch, for example, recognizes "differing forms of time-reckoning."[19] Gurvitch took his lead from "Einstein's general theory of relativity and quantum physics" and argued that "Einstein demonstrated that in physics there are as many times as there are frames of reference and that the speed of movement is relative to the point of view of the observer who chooses one of these frames of reference"[20] and proposes that there is a multiplicity of times framed in such fields as macrophysics, microphysics, mechanics, thermodynamics, and astronomy. In the same manner, immigrants with different frames of temporal reference may not proceed with the same temporalities as the mainstream based on cultural background. As Sorokin and Merton[21] remind us, "local time systems are qualitative, impressed with distinctly localized meanings." With immigration, these local time systems are made up of qualitatively different temporalities that exist next to each other. Such a plurality may exist between the immigrant group and the mainstream, but also within the immigrant group. Earlier, the Greeks coined two different concepts to explain two different types of time: *chronos*, which is measurable and corresponds to "clock time," and *kairos*, which is "associated with the idea of 'existential time.'"[22]

Halbwachs' notion that each group tends to develop its own collective time adds to the recognition of a plurality of times in a multi-ethnic environment.[23] Because these temporalities have different cultural identities, there may exist a lack of "co-evalness" or even a "discordance" among them.[24] One may think of new years observances that fall at different dates than the mainstream New Year's Day or the day of worship that falls on a different day of the week. One speaks of temporal discordance, and not of incompatibility.

The idea that diasporic communities have their own temporalities also follows Lewis and Weigart's[25] argument that "there are culturally based time structures (day, week, seasons)," and from Coser and Coser,[26] who propose that "time perspective is an integral part of a society's values." In other words, a group's time constitutes a fundamental element of its culture and is not always open to negotiation, even in a situation of exile.

In addition to their disjunctive relations with the hegemonic temporality, diasporic temporalities also have a global component that links them temporally with sites far distant in space. Indeed, the global component of diasporic temporalities feeds that disjuncture. Through international migration, whereby newcomers revive homeland practices, through maintaining relations with the homeland whereby practices are kept alive, and through the motivation of immigrants to practice their culture, diasporic temporalities maintain their differences *vis-à-vis* the mainstream culture, and the mainstream, because it is dealing with both aspects of diasporic temporalities – the global and the local – finds itself unable to totally absorb or assimilate these different subcultures. Diasporic globality informs diasporic temporality and helps prevent the collapse of diasporic temporality into mainstream temporality. Globality becomes a local factor to be reckoned with.

Temporal disjuncture thus cannot be explained by focusing on each diasporic time as if it were internally constructed. The relationship with the mainstream is a factor that influences its internal structure, trajectory, and modus operandi. It is through the relationship with the mainstream that diasporic temporalities both become compatible with it and are able to reproduce themselves as different from it. Multitemporality is then a cornerstone of multiculturalism, and the latter cannot be understood adequately without paying attention to the nature of diasporic time in relation to the mainstream.

Temporal inequalities

The hegemonic day, month, and year as defined by the civil government overshadow all other understandings and interpretations of temporal realities. Dominant time is imposed on subalternized time and supports the hegemony of one group over another. Time identifies, differentiates, subjugates, and stigmatizes the other in his or her position of subalternity or inferiority while reinforcing, elevating, and promoting the dominant sector. Dominant time thus disciplines the time of the other,[27] shaping its content as a form of adaptation to a stratified milieu.[28] The week is one of the temporal sites where this disciplinary power is imposed, where subjugation is experienced, and where conflict is managed or subdued. The battle for emancipation for non-Christians living in the West is obstructed by the organization of the civil week, which reflects the hegemonic position of the dominant Christian culture.

The view that the United States is a multicultural society, however, cannot escape the idea of multicultural sites or times. We find in the United States today a large number of "diasporic calendars" (Jewish,

Muslim, Iranian, Baha'i, Chinese, Julian, Indian, Cambodian, Laotian, Ethiopian, and Thai calendars, to name a few) that are located in the interstices of the Western calendar and that provide diasporic rhythms different from the cadence of American life. In addition to the spatial ghettoization of such ethnic groups, there thus occurs a temporal ghettoization in American society. Sometimes temporal ghettoization coincides with spatial ghettoization, and the ghetto becomes the site where this temporality is behaviorally expressed and where it can be studied. But it is not always the case. This ghettoized temporality can also be found in the interstices of mainstream society. It is in these interstices that one sees that inequality also has a temporal dimension. In its broadest sense, then, this book is concerned with temporal inequality and the prospects for the achievement of time equity in multicultural urban America.

The idea of identifying time as a factor of inequality is not new. In the past, two social formations, France during the French Revolution and the Soviet Union during the heyday of Communist Russia – have attempted to undermine state multiculturalism by reconstructing the secular structure of the civil week with no dominant religious influence, thus attempting to equalize individuals in society in the name of reason and science.[29] The French decadal system and the secular Russian week did not favor any religious group. Jews, Christians, and Muslims could celebrate their day of worship and rest only when determined by the state, thereby putatively solving the conflict between the Sabbath and Sunday as specific days of rest.

These two experiments failed after a few years of experimentation.[30] Temporalities are not easily regulated from the top down, by edict. Instead, they tend to assert themselves against hegemonizing forces. If temporal equality is to be achieved in the United States, as a consequence, it is likely to emerge from the bottom up. For many years, the numerous different ethnic calendars observed by immigrants to the United States were used in "silence" by those who were living in the shadow of mainstream American society. But with the increased understanding of the role that multiculturality plays in American daily life, diasporans are pushing not only for the recognition of their calendars, but also for the acceptance of the different temporalities intrinsic to the daily behavioral expression of their cultural lives. The aim is to move these calendars from their position of subalternity to that of equality in the open democratic space of the mainstream multicultural system. The public recognition of these diasporic temporalities in the United States will necessarily lead to the upgrading of the "native" calendrical system of the homeland at the global level in the international arena of nation-states.

Multicultural definitions of the day, the month, and the year

The definition of the day, month, and year is a contested temporal terrain in multicultural America. It means different things in different ethnic calendars. Thus, multiculturalism implies a plural definition of the day. The Western definition of the day is the clock's definition, mechanical and conventional. It is not directly based on astral notions and goes from midnight to midnight. While the Jewish way of reckoning the day, for example, goes from sunset to sunset, thereby counting as a day a continuous period of darkness (full night) and a continuous period of daylight (full day),[31] the mechanical definition of the day in the Western calendar leads to a blurred definition of the night. It cuts the night into two parts, with the latter part of the previous period of darkness and the early part of the current period of darkness both belonging to the current twenty-four hour day.

The Western month in the solar calendar is also a contested temporal terrain because it does not coincide in length and structure, beginning and ending, with the Jewish and Muslim calendars. In other words, the first of the month in the Western calendar does not correspond to the first of the month in these two calendars. These problems are intrinsic to the incompatibility of the solar and lunar (or even lunisolar) systems of time reckoning.

The yearly cycle is again a contested terrain because the length of the year varies from one calendar to the other. The beginning of some ethnic new years does not coincide with the beginning of the new year in the Gregorian calendar. As we have seen, Chinese Americans celebrate their New Year's Day approximately in late January, Iranian Americans in March, and Jewish Americans in September.

Even the Christian majority in the United States has a liturgical calendar that does not coincide with the civil definition of these temporal sequences. Even more than that, civil society develops different mechanisms to account for the day, month, and year. For example, the day may be longer or shorter according to areas covered by the Sunday laws or whether one is dealing with the civil or criminal code. Likewise, the academic year does not necessarily coincide with the budgetary year, which itself does not coincide with the cycle of the civil year.[32]

In short, the asynchronicity between mainstream time and the temporalities of some diasporic groups is the fundamental characteristic of the temporal relations in the American city. This asynchronicity can be conceived of in three ways. As we will see, from the point of view of those experiencing them, the relations between diasporic and hegemonic temporalities may sometimes appear as the interpenetration of temporal systems, whereby diasporans can move fluidly back and forth between the two. Viewed analytically, however, diasporic temporality appears as a system parallel to the mainstream system. As a distinct parallel system, it can be seen as either in conflict or in harmony with the hegemonic system. Finally, it can be seen as a self-reproducing enclave inside the hegemonic system whose strengths reside in its cohesion or coherence as a cultural system. In all these cases, the fundamental experience of the relations between diasporic and hegemonic temporalities involves crossing temporal borders.

Crossing borders

The superposition or intersection of different calendars imposes the practice of border crossing by those involved in either one. Muslims cross the Jewish weekly borders the same way Jews cross borders to navigate, reorganize, and desacralize the Christian Sunday by engaging in secular work and maintaining it as an ordinary work day. Crossing borders is accomplished through the three groups' awareness of each other's days of rest and worship. Crossing or not crossing borders each has its own set of inconveniences: Associates cannot enjoy fellowship because it is their day of rest, and businesses cannot be patronized because they are not available on that day.

Crossing borders can be seen in two different ways. First, one may cross others' temporal boundaries, Working on Sunday may transgress the temporal borders of those who have to go to church. One may cross others' borders because it is convenient for the crosser (for example, buying from Jewish merchants on Sunday) or simply to help out, as happens in the case of Gentiles ("Sabbath goys") who substitute for Jews on the Sabbath. There is a distinction to be made between the crosser who does it for its convenience, however, and the crosser who tempts others to cross. The person who opens his store on Sunday morning invites Christians to do business with him, enticing them to cross their own Sunday boundaries to find themselves in the secular day that Jews, Muslims, and the civil government construct Sunday to be.

One may also cross one's own temporal borders. This happens, for example, when Sunday is the day before Christmas – when Christmas falls on Monday. Christians are allowed to do business on such a Sunday. Sunday Sabbath keepers thus are allowed by the state to break the Sabbath or to cross the religious boundaries of that day.

There are borders that are erected inside the week. They have both local and global dimensions. We cross them to complete the deployment of the civil or religious week. It becomes natural to do so, hoping that the others will change to adapt to the calendrical system used by the group. Thus, it is those who belong to the dominant week who find it most natural to do so. The subaltern who does so is reminded that, to the mainstream, his or her practices are, at worst, a nuisance, as in the case of the Jew or Muslim who opens his store on Sunday morning, and, at best, can be accommodated, as in the case of the Muslim who works extra time to supplement the hours he spends on Friday at the midday prayer at the mosque.

Crossing borders may also be understood as intersectionality.[33] While economic and political integration brings people into the structural makeup of society, these communities sometimes manage – because of religion – to maintain a rhythm of life whose tempo does not closely coincide with the mainstream tempo. Because these weekly cycles do not coincide, but intersect, it becomes necessary to identify and analyze how the portion of the cycle that manifests its difference reverberates in the rest of the week and how the relations between the cycles influence each other. That intersectionality has its own genealogy: the history of its relations with the mainstream cycle and its adjustment to it.

Intersectionality in this deeper sense implies also the crossing of different logics or intentionalities. Because these weeks are culturally different, with different rhythms and peak days, the temporal logic of one may not necessarily coincide with the logic of the others. Logic has a temporal dimension because it reflects the vision that one has of the temporal world. So the week may embody not simply a difference of time, but also of meaning. Crossing borders entails two intertwined processes: both penetrating and traversing the temporal boundaries of a group. This occurs by enhancing or desacralizing a temporal domain or site and by embodying the meanings attached by the group to its temporalities. These processes are especially visible on a peak day, which becomes a point of juncture among the diverse weeks. In this sense, the sociology of the peak day constitutes the privileged terrain for a sociology of intersectionality.

Hegemonic and subaltern temporalities

A major failure of the project of modernity in its attempt to colonize other people's time and to establish a hegemonic Western time every-where on the globe has been the irreducibility of traditional times associated with religious beliefs and practices. The success of the modern project would have created a worldwide religious crisis of identity over the asynchronicity of its time with ritual practices. That issue of resiliency already came to the fore with the presence of Jews in medieval Europe. One can interpret it as a failure of hegemony or as resistance of a domain that could not be domesticated.

The time project of modernity and the project of temporal moder-nity led to two different outcomes in regard to the Rest.[34] In the colo-nial outcome, Western time was imposed as part of the colonization process.[35] Colonization began as a project civilizing the natives. The time of the colonizers would naturally become the time of the colo-nized so as to domesticate them in the language of subjection, thus transforming them into subjects. Even the countries that were not colonized found it necessary with national independence to adopt Western time or standard time for political and economic relations with the West. Hence Sunday has become a day of rest in most of the non-Western states.

The second outcome is provided by the experience of immigrants from the Rest in the West, which is different from that of the Rest of the West. Here, immigrants are called to maintain temporalities of otherness that are not strictly speaking imposed, since they have the choice to return to their homeland.[36] This fundamental aspect of diasporic temporality engenders a time lag that separates the diaspora from the majority. This separation happens both in terms of structural time, the time it takes to move from noncitizen to citizen, and cultural time, the time it takes to convert from one cultural time to a mainstream cultural time that is largely influenced by Western Christianity. The inability to bridge that gap because of religious beliefs may maintain this diaspora in a position of economic disadvantage if the day of rest and worship does not coincide with mainstream practices. Business profit may be lost because of that temporal dichotomy.

When the issues of temporality and globality are seen from the perspectives of the diasporas, the diasporic community must be viewed as a site where mixed time is experienced daily.[37] By "mixed time," we mean a situation or place where two different tempos exist side by side and are used by the hybrid subject who incarnates them. The subject moves back and forth. For example, if my day of rest and worship is Saturday, I am living on diasporic time when I observe it, and when I return to my factory job on Monday morning, I move into hegemonic time.

Mixed time expresses and symbolizes different logics inside the same system: Western logic versus diasporic logic. The one can complement the other, for example when one is used to attain secular goals and the other to attend religious and cultural goals. Diasporic subjects thus develop a mixed consciousness *vis-à-vis* time, and this mixed consciousness is the hallmark of a successful adaptation process. However, these logics also can be a source of conflict, because people tend to see things differently, imprisoned as they are in their culturally influenced logic.

The phenomenon of mixed time shows that from the standpoint of the diaspora, hegemony has a temporality, but does not have a constant time that is always hegemonic. One may speak of the subversion of the subaltern or the ephemeral subalternization of hegemony. This may be a subjective, rather than an objective assessment. As we will see, hegemonic time is at times pushed on the side in the immigrant enclaves so that subaltern time can be choreographed and celebrated.[38] This is one aspect of the Chinese New Year. During this period, the Chinese put their time forward while relegating hegemonic time or the time of the mainstream to a subordinate position.

Global time and the chronopolis

As we have said, diasporic time gives us a glimpse of the localization of globalization because it is a time that owes its existence not simply to locality, but also to globality. It is the extension and reflection of the homeland cultural time. The negotiation of its time with the mainstream and the ability to perform its time is a major project of the diaspora, one that can obliterate, obstruct, or enhance its survival in the nation. Because of its identity as an extension (homeland) and new creation (locality), diasporic time is a node in a particular global temporal flow. It is a localization of global time that is also the globalization of local time.

The concept of "global time" comes to us from the fields of history and international relations, where it has a meaning different from the way we will use it here. Nevertheless, the history of its use shows the genealogical development that leads to the way in which we have conceptualized it here. According to Modelski,[39]

> The first use of the concept in the social sciences is attributable to Wolfgang Eberhard (1965: 13ff), a macrosociolgist specializing in Chinese history. Eberhard pointed out that while time plays no role in scientific experimentation, world time is a critical factor in social processes. Indeed social forces and social changes cannot be analyzed or compared without regard to their place in world time. Fernand Braudel adopted the French version of this term "Le Temps du Monde" as the title of the third volume of *Civilization and Capitalism* . . . Braudel defines "world time" (1982: 17–18) as "a type of time experienced on a world scale," a "kind of super-structure of world history." . . . It is the "history of the long, even of the very long time span." World time is not to be understood as accounting for all of human existence, but it does track structural change: the major transformations in world politics, economics, society, and culture.

For Laidi, the concept of global time (*temps mondial*) must not simply be defined within the context of linear historicity, but must also account for shifts in world history and world-historical consciousness. In this light, the globalization process needs not only to be contextualized, but temporized, as well. For him, global time can be defined as "the moment when all the geopolitical and cultural consequences of the post cold war become intertwined with the progression ('acceleration') of the processes of economic, social and cultural globalization."[40] This perspective has its strengths in the way in which it identifies the role of world events in the social construction of global time.

In a comment on Laidi's view on global time, Virilio[41] argues that we have passed from a notion of time based on the movement of our planet around the sun, which leads to the distinction between day and night, to an axial or global notion of time that shapes all local times. As he puts it, "all local times are dominated by global time."[42]

Giddens[43] equates globalization with the worldwide standardization of temporal measurement and the consequent universalization of time. It is a time that reverberates in the hegemonic calendrical reference system without eliminating subalternized local ethnic or religious calendars. His concern is with "time–space distanciation," a dissembedding process by which "the 'lifting out' of social relations from local contexts of interaction and their restructuring across indefinite spans of time-space" occurs.[44] He sees this process not as genuine to postmodernity, but rather as a consequence of modernity.

In contrast to Giddens, Harvey provides a discussion of the globalization of time in the context of not only modernity, but also postmodernity. But like Giddens, he is also interested in space–time relations.[45] Where Giddens sees this in terms of "time–space distanciation," Harvey argues rather for "time–space compression" to suggest how space has been annihilated through the compression of time and how the shrinking of space necessarily leads to the presentification of time. He ties his explanation to recent shifts in modes of capital accumulation.

Global time has also been seen as the outcome of the standardization of time.[46] The standardization of time – with the imposition of metric time, Greenwich time, and standard time – has contributed to the delocalization and mechanization of local time. This decontextualization of local time is seen to be an important element in the architectural infrastructure of world time. While Luhmann[47] conceives of world time as an abstract mechanism that reconciles and harmonizes different temporal systems of modern societies, Adam sees it as a basic infrastructure that feeds and sustains the globalization process. She notes that:

since the beginning of this century, time has been standardized and globalized while the worldwide net of wireless and electronic communication brought about the global present. At 10:00 A.M., 1 July 1913, the Eiffel Tower transmitted the first time signal that synchronized time across the globe. Wireless signals travelling at near the speed of light displaced variable local times and imposed instead one uniform, hegemonic world time for all . . . The globalized rationalization of time and the creation of global simultaneity can thus be seen as integral components of the wider globalization strategies of this country.[48]

Castells[49] is perhaps the first who provided the ingredients for a "global time geography." He refers to global time as "timeless time," which is "the emerging, dominant form of social time in the network society."[50] For him, timeless time (which also includes virtual time) "occurs when the characteristics of a given context, namely, the informational paradigm and the network society, induce systemic perturbations in the sequential order of phenomena performed in that context."[51]

In this book, we refer to "global time" as the duration and moment during which a diaspora, its homeland, and other sites are interconnected or interact with each other, allowing the diasporans to keep alive their transnational cultural identity. Global time refers to sectoral practices, as well as to the plurality of practices of a diaspora. This plurality within global time seems to reflect the diasporic condition.

Thus we conceive of global time as the duration in which members of a transnational group or network are in interaction or communion with each other. Transnational time then becomes the duration in which local and extraterritorial sites are connected and through which global time is effected. Global time recognizes the multiplicity of practices and domains linked to each other through transnational connections that give different identities to duration. This conceptualization of global time recognizes its differentiation and stratification, as well as its internal plurality. Global time is thus sustained by different transnational infrastructures or different infrastructural architectures.

Transnational time links two or more nations to each other. What we might call "transnationality" thus would indicate the level of intensity of these connections and their importance in an hierarchy of scale.[52] However, we need an additional concept that enables us to map the terrain or geography of connectivity and the various sets and subsets of the network. We need a concept that encompasses the global scale of the interaction. "Transglobality" assumes that the world is made up of a number of globalities that intersect and crisscross, but do not coincide because these global networks have their own orientation.

With transglobality we acknowledge the limit of transnationality, respatializing it inside this larger framework, subalternizing it as the vehicle through which globality is materialized, and temporizing it to account for the temporalities of global chronopolises. Transglobality further indicates two types of motion: the crisscrossing of the multiple sites of a same global domain, as in the case of the practice of Islam and the transnational relations it generates between the homeland and diasporic sites, and the border crossing of different global domains. And of course these practices can be achieved on a smaller or larger scale of globality.[53]

Transglobality brings about a new understanding of the world by putting the emphasis on the twin factors of globality and locality. In a situation where the locale is understood to be globalized, globalized locality and localized globality are engines through which the global factor can be deciphered. The global – wherever it is – is localized. In this scheme of things, the relations between the global and the local end up being relations between a localized globality and globalized locality. In such a perspective, the parameters of these globalized relations can be mapped and the relations inside such a domain considered as transglobal as well as those across domains.

The concept of transglobality allows us to unveil the grammatical rules that are at the foundation of the chronopolis as a transglobal social formation. The "chronopolises," a term coined from the Greek *chronos* and *polis*, are societal entities that use similar temporal rhythms that differentiate them from each other. Transglobality indicates that as a transglobal formation, the chronopolis is not simply involved in local diasporic time, but in a time that also has tentacles in other areas of the world. Through a multiplex of transnational relations, this transglobality has an infrastructure. Decoding and analyzing the global infrastructure of the chronopolis is part of the exercise of this book.

In New York, there are several such units that maintain a rhythm of life different from that of the mainstream community. I refer to such entities as "chronopolises" to imply the uniqueness of their temporal makeup and the differences they exhibit in the daily life of the city. Since these entities are diasporized, they are in temporal harmony with the homeland and other diasporic sites, but sometimes in temporal disharmony with mainstream New York. I also call them "chronopolises" to accentuate these transnational linkages and their different rhythms of life and to recognize them as extensions of homeland time, the official and dominant time of the secular state or the unofficial but dominant time of a given religion.[54] Thus, "chronopolization" is the process by which an immigrant group constitutes itself as an enclave city, maintains ongoing transnational relations with extraterritorial sites, displays in some important areas of social life a temporal orientation visibly distinct from the mainstream, and uses the trajectory of its cultural time as one of the fundamental principles of its social organization and the mechanism that regulates aspects of its relations with the rest of society.

A chronopolis is a transglobalized local community that follows a rhythm of life that is at times dissimilar to that of the social milieu where it is incorporated, but similar to the extraterritorial sites to which it is transnationally connected. Such disjunctures may be occasional, such as those caused by the celebration of specific holidays or holy days (flag day, independence day), or permanent because of the use of a different calendrical system (lunar, lunisolar), or a different week structure (the Jewish or Muslim week). Members of a chronopolis differ from those who reside in one time zone, but live according to the rhythm of life of another time zone, as happens in the case of stockbrokers who live in London or Jerusalem and who must follow closely the mood on Wall Street.

The chronopolis is unlike the transglobal "ethnopolis." While the latter is based on ethnicity, the former is not dependent on such an identification.[55] While ethnicity is a major factor for some chronopolises, such as Chinatown, it is not the principal element for others, such as Muslims, who must follow the Islamic calendar irrespective of their place of birth. The categories "chronopolis" and "ethnopolis" are not necessarily mutually exclusive, however. There are ethnopolises – again, Chinatown is an example – that are also chronopolises because of the different yearly cycles that cadence the rhythm of their social lives. As a chronopolis, diasporic tempo-rality participates in a network of temporal connections that go beyond the realm of the homeland precisely because these religious and cultural times go beyond the realm of ethnicity and national-ity.[56] No doubt the connections with homeland time are paramount in intensity, but that same homeland has always been part of a larger network of time practices because of its religious practices. For this reason, the chronopolis cannot be reduced purely to an ethnopolis, where ethnicity is the dominant factor.

The global chronopolis

The argument that I am articulating in this book is not simply that these polar temporal entities have a global dimension or orientation, but they are indeed enclaved global cities, and as such the local expression of their existence has been shaped by the subaltern posi-tion of their incorporation in the American city. They are not simply local entities. They are internally shaped by the global currents that are an intrinsic characteristic of their makeup, and time is a prin-ciple of the social organization of their constitution. They are global cities, as well. As a form of *polis*, chronopolises are cities that have a tempo distinct from other cities. Thus, the global city is made up of a number of temporal social formations that have their own distinct global orientations.

The chronopolis is a subaltern city whose inhabitants periodically retreat from the mainstream tempo of work, leisure, and rest to main-tain the rhythmic weekly cadence of their cultural communities. As a consequence of this form of immigrant adaptation, the mainstream week is very flexible to diasporic change as activities that do not coin-cide with its tempo are introduced in its interstices. Such trans-national communities are engaging in a back-and-forth motion, hybridizing for their own sake those moments that coincide with mainstream time and singularizing those that are elements of culture-bound diasporic time. Such culture-bound temporal practices are markers that indicate when the community is available and when it is not. For example, one sees Muslims pulling their children out of school on Islamic holy days and Orthodox Jewish merchants closing their shops on Saturday.

The chronopolis is a city with a different religious temporality, a different weekly peak day, and a different business week cycle. It is a city that is intertwined with the mainstream city, but whose distinct temporality identifies its difference. It is a city in temporal motion whose ebb and flow keeps it from being totally absorbed by the mainstream.

What makes the study of the chronopolis important is the temporal disharmony that distinguishes it from the larger city, that localizes the globality of its existence, and that sustains the dynamic of its relations with the city and with the homeland and other diasporic sites. Thus, temporality becomes a strategic variable or angle through which multicultural components of the global city and the globalization of transnational communities can be studied. In this light, time is conceptualized and operationalized as a corollary of space and is seen as a pivotal element in the architectural makeup of the global city.

2
Hegemonic and Subaltern Temporalities in New York

It may not be obvious to the casual observer that the "civil Sunday" is not identical to the "Christian Sunday," since for both, Sunday is a day of rest. This is why it is important to investigate their separate identities, even though they tend to cover the same temporal domain. This overlapping is part of the historical process whereby the civil Sunday provides a legal shield for the Christian Sunday, which itself is used as a barometer to gauge the moral and spiritual life of the population. The Christian and civil Sundays are each hegemonic in their own sphere. However, when compared with each other, the civil Sunday emerges as hegemonic, and the Christian Sunday as subaltern. These two temporalities are inserted or incorporated in the daily life of the city and influence its social shape in different ways. The Christian and civil Sundays in fact reflect the reality of two epistemic communities whose public spheres, spatial boundaries, and activities do not necessarily coincide.[1] Attempts to use the Christian Sunday to control the civil Sunday have failed for the same reasons that attempts to use the civil Sunday to control the Christian Sunday have failed: As we will see, these local entities are part of global networks that cannot be controlled locally because of their transnational tentacles.

The best single set of data that provides empirical evidence for the study of the construction of the civil week is found in the blue laws. Since the blue laws are heavily focused on defining Sunday as a civil day, the day of enforced rest, they indirectly help to identify the boundaries of the civil week, the distinction between work days and rest days, and the distinction between the civil Sunday and the

Christian Sunday. For reasons of expediency, this chapter will not concentrate on all the blue laws in the United States, state by state, but rather on the evolution of this practice in New York City, since its Jewish population was a main target of religious discrimination and was one of the groups radically affected by the blue laws. These New York laws help us to disclose the genealogy of the definition of the "civil Sunday," the "civil day," and indirectly, the "civil week."

The phrase "blue laws" refers to legislation concocted in the American colonies to regulate permissible activities deemed to be compatible with the Lord's Day. Where the expression comes from is a matter of debate among historians. Two explanations pertaining to the phrase "blue laws" seem to be prominent in historical research. One refers to the color of the paper used to print such laws. For example, Hinman argues that "the term 'blue laws,' attached to this early code of laws, is said to have originated from the fact the first printed laws in the New Haven colony were enveloped in blue colored paper."[2] The other view states that "blue laws" was used to refer to the strictness with which they were applied, the constancy with which they were upheld, and the fidelity with which they were followed. As Trumbull explains, "to be 'blue' was to be 'puritanic,' precise in the observance of legal and religious obligations, rigid, gloomy, over-strict."[3]

The blue laws originated in Europe and migrated to the United States during the colonial period, as they did to other colonized territories. They were part of the extension of the metropolitan sphere of influence. At their inception in the United States, they were global entities and were responsible for the global patterning of Sunday. The globalizing tendency of Christendom and the Western hegemonic week universalized the norms for Sunday, with local variations set by the legislature and local practices. They thus were not simply local laws, although they had a local goal.

In the modern blue laws as enacted in New York State, the state polices its civil week by policing secular activities on the Lord's Day. In the process, it accentuates the temporal clusters of the week: working days and the day of rest. It regulates the hours of work, dividing the day into routine working hours and overtime hours, an earlier distinction that modern life has made more flexible.

The state identifies and distinguishes between types of labor allowed or disallowed on Sunday. For example, selling milk is fine, but selling liquor is not. It also defines when labor is permitted within the day of rest. Some types of labor are allowed before 11:00 a.m. and other types after 2:00 p.m., for example, selling beer in a super-market for off-premises use. It produces a hierarchy of spaces, as well: Some activities are allowed in some areas and not in others within the same state. Cities are endowed with rights to police Sunday activities by local ordinances. The policing of Sunday activities is said to be carried out to allow Christians to attend to their religious obligations, to prevent disorder at night (liquor restrictions after 11:00 p.m. on Saturday), and to protect the Christian majority from possible excesses of non-Christian diasporas.

This chapter's focus on the blue laws is a way to problematize the civil week by contrasting it with the Christian week, showing its hegemonic identity, its genealogical development, its structural relations with the other weekly cycles, how it permeates everyday life, and how it must be seen as a local node in a transglobal network of temporality. It shows the ways in which the civil week, because it provides a rhythm to transnational economic transactions, international relations, and border-crossing practices, plays a pivotal role in the institutional, familial, and individual life of New York City. It further demonstrates how the construction of this temporality affects and is affected by the other religious and virtual weekly cycles and how local and global factors have contributed to its present shape. In other words, this chapter attempts to unpack some constitutive elements of the civil week by focusing on civil Sunday in order to develop a theory that explains its hegemonic position in the temporal universe of New York – the hegemonic position with which all subaltern temporalities must in one way or another deal.

Diasporization as hegemonization

One can follow with ease the genealogy of the formation of the hegemonic temporalities generated by the relations between the civil week and the Christian week from the emergence of the early Christian church from Judaism through the migration of Christians from the Roman Empire to England and thereafter to the American colonies.[4] The Christian Sunday as we know it today developed its European identity before the British colonization of the American territories.[5] This identity emanates from the disentangling of the Christian Sabbath from the Jewish Sabbath as a series of diasporizations.[6]

The disembedding of the Christian Sabbath from the Jewish Sabbath began before the shaping of the identity of civil Sunday with Constantine's edict of 321.[7] Church historians spoke of it as the era of "deJudaization" or even as an "anti-Judaism of differentiation."[8] The separation of Sabbaths was a source of tension between the Church of Rome dominated by Gentile Christians (Roman Catholicism or Western Christianity) and the Church of Jerusalem dominated by Jewish Christians (the Orthodox Church or Eastern Christianity). The Orthodox Church continued to observe the Jewish Sabbath and also met on the first day of the week for corporate worship.[9] Bacchiocchi argues that "the adoption of Sunday observance in place of the Sabbath did not occur in the primitive church of Jerusalem by virtue of the authority of Christ or of the Apostles, but rather took place several decades later, seemingly in the Church of Rome."[10] In that sense, Roman Christianity is fundamentally a diasporic religion. The diasporic church's attempt to impose itself on the homeland led to the schism between the Roman Church and the Eastern Orthodox Church.

The Christian Sabbath is different from the Jewish Sabbath not simply in terms of different days of worship, but also in terms of the definition of the day. The theological justification for the Jewish Sabbath is based on the story of creation as told in the book of Genesis in the Old Testament, and the justification for the other is based on the story of the resurrection of Jesus as reported in the Gospels in the New Testament and the rest required for that day.[11]

For Zerubavel, the identification of Sunday as a peak day is explained in terms of marking the boundaries of the new faith to specify its distinctness and its different identity.[12] For Luther, it was the church authorities who established it to entice the unity of the group.[13] For Bacchiocchi, it is the imperialism of the Church of Rome over the Church of Jerusalem.[14] For mainstream Catholic theology, it is the memorial of the resurrection of Jesus and the prefiguration of Resurrection Day.[15]

The identification of Christian Sunday as a rest day does not emanate from the primitive church, since believers were not prevented from working on that day. It is a late tradition that took its present shape in the sixth century. According to Rordorf, "until well into the second century we do not find the slightest indication in our sources that Christians marked Sunday by any kind of absten- tion from work."[16] Huber further remarks that "in the Latin fathers of this period we meet absolutely no law about rest from work on Sunday . . . It was in the sixth century that the Sabbath command- ment first became an important part of the justification of rest from work on Sunday."[17] In other words, it was neither a biblical nor a church obligation to rest on Sunday. It was not until the sixth century that such an injunction appeared in canon law as a policy of the Catholic Church.

Ward informs us that "Sunday laws came to England with the coming of the missionary Augustine and the conversion of the Saxon kings."[18] Porter also reminds us that "the American Sunday is quite naturally the off-shoot of the British . . . In New York . . . Anglicanism influenced social customs and church-going is frequently followed by agreeable gatherings of friends and neighbors."[19] The civil week as we know it in New York City thus is the outcome of the dias- porization of the weekly structure that was already in existence in England during what we might call the "retemporization" period, when the Native American territories were transformed into British colonies. British time – later, Western time, with the adoption of the Gregorian calendar in 1752 in the American colonies – was imposed on Native American hosts and guest-settlers alike.[20] In the process, the guests and hosts were being drawn slowly under the umbrella of this hegemonic diasporic time. The temporal reframing of the American colonies was necessary in order to relocate hosts and guests inside a new temporal order where they were called upon to remold their social identities. Territorial colonization went hand in hand with temporal colonization. Both contributed to transformational changes in the identity structures of the newly subalternized and hegemonized groups. The Christian Sunday thus was incorporated in New York as a diasporic institution or a diaspora of a diaspora. It is diasporic in the sense that it is a carryover from England, links local practices to European practices, and is spiritually linked to a "center" – Israel.

Hegemonization could be achieved to the extent that other people's time could be colonized and that the time of the dominant group could be imposed as the hegemonic time of the territory or nation. This outcome could not be achieved by brute force alone.

Diasporization must be seen not only in terms of people, but also in terms of institutions, because hegemonic diasporas create local institutions to help sustain their dominant identities.[21] The institutional matrix provides the infrastructure for diasporic practices because local institutions or temporalities are linked transnationally and transglobally to headquarters institutions. In this case, a legal mechanism had to be set in place to provide the justification and frame of reference for such an undertaking. That is how the blue laws came into being as a system of colonial practice. They were diasporized to serve as a legal reference in the construction of the civil week and of civil Sunday as a day of rest that is also the peak day of the week.

Since these laws were developed by the Anglo-Protestant majority, they reflect foremost the preoccupations of this group: the articulation of the work week with the Christian Sabbath. Subaltern faiths, however, have been less impressed by the coalescence of two dominant identities – civil and Christian – in the same day. Such an occurrence further contributed to the double subjugation of both Jewish and Muslim diasporic communities by the Anglo majority and the temporal assimilation of even those who have different diasporic identities: They are subalternized *vis-à-vis* the dominant day of rest, which prevents them from working on Sunday, and because of their faith, *vis-à-vis* Christianity, the dominant religion.

The coalescence of the civil and the Christian week enforced by the blue laws likewise serves the interests of the racial state. Time is racialized in such a way that it serves as an infrastructural vehicle for the flow of practices that sustain and feed the state. Minority status requires minoritized space and time as the context or infrastructure for its performance. The week is a good example of racialization because its temporal frame is arbitrary. It is not a function of astral motions, as in the case of the day or the month, and is molded to empower the dominant Christian group.

The racial state could not prosper without the racialization of space and time. Space is racialized to encode the hegemony of the dominant group, the same way time is racialized to reflect the subalternization of the minoritized groups.[22] The racialized temporal logic that the state maintains accomplishes both the hegemony of the dominant and the subjugation of the subjugated. That is, it places one group ahead of the others and imposes a temporal stratification system at the expenses of subaltern groups. The racialization of the week was a foundational process because its inscription subalternized the temporal cycles of minoritized groups.

The racialization of time sustains the structure of inequality that forms the architecture of American society. The racialization of time feeds the hegemonic–subaltern relations of segments of the population. In other words, racialization of time is an important variable in the production of inequality, but also contributes to the creation of a heterogeneous structure of inequality. For Hanchard, "racial time is defined as the inequalities of temporality that result from power relations between racially dominant and subordinate groups. Unequal relationships between dominant and subordinate groups produce unequal temporal access to institutions, goods, services, resources, power, and knowledge, which both groups recognize . . . Time, when linked to relations of dominance and subordination, is another social construct that marks inequality between various social groups."[23]

The day and the week in the civil calendar

The coalescence of the civil and the Christian week enforced by the blue laws provides the temporal context in which the subalternized and racialized identity of non-Christian believers or unbelievers is expressed. Like it or not, it is the temporal sequence that structures and guides their daily life.

The civil week does not coincide with any of the other weekly cycles, Jewish, Muslim, or other. The civil week, however, overlaps with these weekly cycles. And although the dominant civil week is influenced by the Christian week, it is, nevertheless, not identical to it. As we have said, it disciplines the Christian week, although not, perhaps, with the same rigidity as it does the other weeks. At the same time, one must recognize that the Christian week provides an infrastructure for the civil week. It provides the hegemonic secular week system with direction and meaning.

The civil week shapes the rhythms of the other weekly cycles as it subdivides itself in terms of workdays, weekends, and a rest day. In this construction, Saturday could go one way or the other. It is seen as part of the weekend, or as a continuation of the work week, or simply as the day of preparation preceding Sunday, the day of rest and worship.

Although influenced by the Christian week structure, the civil week has its own shape and meaning. It is the week that sustains the activities of hegemonic civil society and government. It is a week molded on the deployment of the civil year, with its tempos, direction, and symbolism. The beginning and ending of the civil week varies, depending on the domain. For the purpose of regulating the official day of rest, Sunday is identified as "the first day of the week" (General Business Law art. 2). In contrast, Monday becomes the first day of the week in labor law (art. 519), and employers are allowed to use any day of the week as the day of rest: A day of rest "consist[s] of at least twenty-four consecutive hours of rest in each and every calendar week" (p. 29).[24] To show that the identity of the civil week is different from that of the Christian one, the state thus Balkanizes and further subalternizes the rest day of non-Christians and deploys a new hierarchy of rest days that serves as an infrastructure and sustains the hierarchy of status in society.[25]

The peak day of the civil week

In addition to Sunday, the peak day of the hegemonic civil and Christian weeks, the subaltern weekly cycles within the American week each have a peak day. It is erroneous to assume that these peak days all carry the same meaning or refract the same way on the rest of the week. These peak days originate at different times and were inserted in the history of the republic at different periods.

For one thing, "peak day" means different things for the civil week and the religious week, including the Christian week. While Christians and Jews speak of their peak day of the week as the day of worship and rest, Muslims speak of the day when worship occurs. The latter also speak of the hours of the day (midday) when communal worship is obligatory. In Judaism, the entire peak day is holy, and although it may be preferable to hold congregational worship at certain hours, worship is not restricted to any specific hours, as it is for Muslims.

Although the peak day of the Christian week was observed early on in the American colonies because of the Western European origin of the colonists, it was not until the ratification of the United States Constitution that there was a sustained effort to separate the Christian week from the civil week and therefore the Christian

Sunday from the civil Sunday.[26] By the late twentieth century, the civil Sunday had emerged, with its distinctive features and peculiarities.

In contrast, the Jewish Sabbath had to struggle for recognition by the mainstream, and its history remains that of a subalternized peak day.[27] As we will see in the next chapter, this peak day inserts itself inside the hegemonic week, recovers its strengths in this peripheral position, carves a niche for itself in the interstices of the dominant system, and, in the process, competes for recognition, legitimacy, and equality under the law.

The Muslim Friday is still more peripheralized as a peak day, partly because the visible presence of Muslims in New York City is of more recent origin and partly because, as we will see in the chapter after that, their peak day is not a day of rest.[28]

What each peak day – Friday for Muslims, Saturday for Jews, and Sunday for Christians – has in common with the others is that it is a day of communal devotion or congregational prayer, the day when public worship is mandatory for the believers and practitioners of these faiths. For Christians, the peak day is the first day of the week, while for the Jews, it is the seventh, or last day of the week. As a first day for the Christians, the peak day could not be easily justified as a day of rest. Rest from what? By emphasizing the first day as the memorial of the resurrection of Jesus, the Christians emphasize communal worship over rest, while in selecting Sunday as its peak day, the civil week emphasizes rest over worship, since the civil week is neutral on this foundational theological issue. Since the Muslims do not mandate a day of rest, their selection of the penultimate day of the Muslim week is not fraught with the same kinds of theological problems of interpretation in relation to those encumbered by the first day of the Christian week.

Although the peak day means different things to different faiths and to civil society, it remains – for all – a special day that is set apart from the rest of the week. It stops the routine of the week, stops all activities for a day or a couple of hours – all at once – and returns to the routine of daily life thereafter. This moment of respite from daily work is supposed to reenergize people physically, spiritually, or both for the coming week. It is the day to which the week leads or from which the week begins. It is the alpha for some and omega for others.

A comparative analysis of these peak days also reveals that not all of them are on an equal footing. They are placed in a hierarchy of positions, with the civil week's peak day in a hegemonic position, followed closely by the Christian peak day. The other peak days are peripheralized and subalternized not only because they fall on another day, but because they are held by minority groups. It is also worth noting that these peak days do not have the same beginning and ending time: Some start at sundown, others at midnight.

The civil Sunday in New York State: The blue laws

The civil Sunday as it is presently constructed by the blue laws in New York State is seemingly straightforward, but as its genealogy shows, that appearance is deceiving. The most recent statues pertaining to Sunday legislation were issued in New York in 1985.[29] They refer to Sunday as a day of rest and place restrictions on some retail trades to prevent "serious interruptions of the repose and religious liberty of the community" (p. 6). The laws do not endorse any religion, but are issued in the name of religious liberty, in reference, one may suppose, to the First Amendment of the Constitution. The break from the Christian week could not be more direct, yet at the same time, the overlap between the day of "repose" and the Christian Sabbath means that the separation of church and state is undermined here.

The blue laws provide the parameters within which the construction of civil Sunday is effected. The law sets the character of the day. "The first day of the week being by general consent set apart for rest and religious uses, the law prohibits the doing on that day of certain acts" (p. 6). Its civil purpose is "to promote public morals and good order" (*ibid.*). Such a law falls within the realm of "the public policy of the state [which] is to set aside Sunday as a day of repose" (p. 7). In doing so, the legislature, we are told, does not act on behalf of any religion, but rather "within its general police powers" (p. 7). Furthermore, it is said that the legislature did not create such a law, but that it has been part of the general practice of common law. In this rationale, "the Sabbath exists as a day of rest by common law, and without the necessity of legislative action to establish it; the legislature merely regulates its observance" (p. 7).

By using "Sabbath" to refer to the peak day of the civil week, the meaning of the word in the New York Sunday legislation no longer coincides with the temporal sequence it is supposed to identify. The word "Sabbath" means "the seventh day," "the day of rest," and "the day of worship" in its pristine Jewish definition. In its Christian form, "the first day of the week" is substituted for "the seventh day." Here, it means only "the first day of the week" and "the day of rest."

Thus, the definition of the Lord's Day is conventionalized. However, as with most conventions in the realm of praxis, there is no homogeneity of the civil Sunday in New York. The day frequently has been fractured to meet different personal and institutional needs. The civil Sunday expands or contracts, depending on the nature of the policy the state was putting forward. Its construction also varies over time, which again indicates its conventionality and the flexibility of its boundaries. Over the past hundred years or so, the civil Sunday has been thoroughly fractured in terms of time, space, and social practices, not just within New York State, but between states across the nation.

The list of such fractures is long. There has been an evolution from one era to another, mirroring changes in civil society. The Sunday laws of 1883 prohibited the practice of all public sports on the first day of the week, while the law of 1985 stipulates that "it shall be lawful to conduct, witness, participate or engage in any form of public sports, exercises or shows which are conducted or engaged in primarily for the entertainment of spectators . . . on the first day of the week after five minutes past one o'clock in the afternoon."[30]

More importantly, however, the state has increasingly recognized that its previous forms of discrimination have been based on temporal exclusion, and, following changes in society, it has evolved adherence to a policy of multicultural inclusion based on a multicultural definition of Sunday. Since the state's declared interest increasingly has been in keeping order and peace during the weekly day of rest, it allows non-Christian individuals to use any day of the week as a day of rest. Instead of being centripetal and exclusionary, now Sunday is centrifugal and inclusionary. We are in a regime in which the day of rest is no longer imposed by the state, and the state acknowledges and recognizes the irreducibility of other days as such. Sunday thus has been transformed from sole temporal site of rest to the hegemonic site, since its status is tied to the will of the majority, and Saturday has gained in status from an ordinary working day in the rest of the week to an alternative and subaltern day of rest for Jews.

The blue laws thus have been applied differently in reference to different groups or institutions. The Sunday laws do not apply equally to Christians and Jews. Provisions are made to allow Jews to carry on their activities on Sunday and to take Saturday as their Sabbath. "It is a sufficient defense to a prosecution for work or labor on the first day of the week that the defendant uniformly keeps another day of the week as holy time, and does not labor on that day, and that the labor complained of was done in such manner as not to interrupt or disturb other persons observing the first day of the week as holy time."[31] This injunction has several implications: It recognizes religious freedom, including the authority of religions to establish a day of worship for the faithful and to accommodate those who use another day of rest; it recognizes the multiculturality of Sunday (a day of rest for some and a working day for others) and it hegemonizes Sunday and subalternizes other days of rest. The blue laws not only accommodate another day as Sabbath to suit the needs of the Jewish population, but they also accommodate another definition of the day. They stipulate that "the term 'day of the week' as used in this section, shall mean and include the period of time of not less than twenty-four consecutive hours *commencing at or before sundown on one day and terminating at or after sundown on the following day.*"[32]

There have been differences in the application of Sunday laws because of their lack of agreement with the General Business Law and General Municipal Law, or even because of the lack of agreement between the ways in which the civil and criminal code construct Sunday. The following clause alludes to the possibility of conflict in the application of the Sunday laws: "No provision of this section shall be construed to prohibit any owner from doing business seven days a week, where any other general, special or local law, rule or regulation does not specifically prohibit such activity."[33]

There have been differences in the application of the same body of law to similar practices (labor, processions). "All processions and parades on Sunday in any city, excepting only funeral processions for the actual burial of the dead, and processions to and from a place of worship in connection with a religious service there celebrated, are forbidden; and in such excepted case there shall be no music, fireworks, discharge of cannon or firearms, or other disturbing noise. At a military funeral, or at the funeral of a United States soldier, sailor or marine, or of a national guardsman . . . or of an employee of the national, state, and municipal governments, music may be played while escorting the body."[34]

There also have been differences in the position of Sunday *vis-á-vis* other holidays. The Sunday before Christmas or the New Year is a "day of exception" endowed with a "special day status." In these circumstances, one is allowed to do business as if it were a regular business day. These days of exception are such that the civil identity of the day takes precedence over its religious or Christian identity. This is a key example whereby civil Sunday imposes its hegemonic civil identity over the subaltern identity of Christian Sunday.

There even have been differences in the temporal identity of Sunday: "a day in law" for the blue laws and not a day in law for Construction Law (p. 21), meaning that it cannot be computed as a regular day. It is stated in the General Construction Law that in the computation of time, "Sunday cannot for the purpose of performing a contract be regarded as a day in law, and when it is due on Sunday, performance on Monday following is in time."[35] It is further stated in relation to expiration of lease that "where the last day of the term occurred on a Sunday, the tenant could remove from the premises on the following day without incurring liability as a 'hold over tenant.'"[36] Likewise, a provision is included that states "if any bill shall not be returned by the governor within ten days, Sundays excepted, after it shall have been presented to him, the same shall be a law in like manner, as if he had signed it" (p. 139).

There likewise have been different definitions of the day in terms of the legality of beginning and ending any activity and the legal dilemmas that the identity of the day creates. Can work initiated on Saturday be completed on Sunday? Can work be initiated on Sunday in order to complete it during the week? When we contract someone to work for us, can we compute Sunday in the number of days? If we have to pay our rent on the first of each month, and the first is a Sunday, should we pay on Saturday or on the following Monday?

There have been different applications of the blue laws within the State of New York. For example, the Sunday laws of 1895 bracketed New York State into two categories: places where its clause on barbering applied and places where it did not. This clause stipulates that "any person who carries on or engages in the business of shaving, hair cutting, or other work of a barber on the first day of the week, shall be deemed guilty of a misdemeanor." The clause also contains the following provisions: "Provided, that in the city of New York, and the village of Saratoga Springs, barber shops or other places where a barber is engaged in shaving, hair cutting, or other work of a barber may be kept open, and the work of a barber may be performed therein until one o'clock of the afternoon of the first day of the week."[37]

Just as there has been no homogeneous civil Sunday in New York, there has been no "federal Sunday" that is identical everywhere in the United States in terms of actual time and in terms of what is permissible. The national Sunday is fractured by different state practices.

It is fractured, first of all, in terms of the length of the day. The temporal boundaries of civil Sunday are not identical from one state to another. For example, in 1897, the state of New Mexico defined Sunday as "the time between sunrise and midnight of said day."[38] In 1883, North Carolina defined Sunday as "that portion of the day between sunrise and sunset."[39] For the Penal Laws of Hawaii in 1897, it was defined as "the time between midnight preceding and the midnight following the same day."[40]

It is also fractured in terms of exceptions for types of labor permitted. In Kentucky in 1903, "work required in the maintenance or operation of a ferry, steamboat, or steam or street railroads" was allowed on Sunday, while in New York in 1901, "all labor on Sunday is prohibited, except works of necessity or charity."[41]

Finally, it is fractured in terms of exceptions for ages of laborers above 14 or 15 years old. In 1907, Nebraska criminalized any person 14 years old or over who worked on Sunday, and in 1902, South Carolina did the same to any resident of the state 15 years old or over.[42]

The blue laws as boundaries

From a constitutional standpoint, the blue laws were not enacted to define the Christian Sunday, but rather to define the civil Sunday, since the state has no authority to pass laws regarding the former. Hence, the paradox is that the blue laws were passed to provide a temporal niche for Christian Sunday, since they were about the separation of the Christian Sunday from the civil Sunday. The definition of the Christian Sunday and the civil Sunday are to be found in the interstices set by the blue laws that separate the one from the other. The blue laws thus are about boundary maintenance, contraction, and expansion.[43]

The blue laws define the boundaries, but not the internal content of the Christian and civil Sundays. This is why it is important to focus on the edges or boundaries that separate these two systems of time reckoning. The first set of boundaries established by the blue laws prevents transgressions of the Christian Sunday by those who observe the civil Sunday. In effect, they are negative laws, in contrast to positive laws – that is, they legislate or stipulate what we cannot or are not allowed to do, not what we must do. The intent of the state has been to restrict activities that undermine both rest and worship on Sunday.

The second set of boundaries the law defines have to do with the contours of the day and how the day can be expanded or reduced, depending on what the state wants to accomplish. Here one also sees much variation in the content or length of the day. The civil Sunday is variable. For some, this also has been true of the Christian Sunday since the Second Vatican Council allowed Catholics to fulfill their Sunday obligations by attending church on Saturday, beginning in the afternoon. This partly explains the lack of mutual relations between the civil and Christian Sundays.

The third set of boundaries refers to the meaning of the day, the way it is differentiated. Is it a day like any other day, or is it a different day? In what ways is it different and the same? Sunday is the most hybrid of all the days of the week because it has features that make it similar to the other days and characteristics that make it different from the other days. This is a day that is included in the computation of the month, but that is not counted as a day in some labor contracts. One may say that it has a special status in the week.

The fourth set of boundaries points to Sunday's global status. Sunday resonates as a day of rest everywhere on the globe. However, it does not have this status everywhere. So it is in this sense once again a circumscribed type of globality. It is a day that sets limits to global economic transactions, and thus disciplines the working behavior of the week worldwide.

The last boundaries define the nature of the beginning and ending of the week. The civil week begins on Sunday and is referred to as "the first day of the week." As we have seen, the first day thus ends up being a day of rest, in contrast with the first day of the Jewish week.

These boundaries, however, are far from impermeable. The state has redefined Sunday to indicate the period of time when work in general is forbidden and the type of work in particular that is allowed.[44] However, the interpretation of "work" and "rest" is, for many, subjective. In the traditional sense, "rest" signifies that no work should be performed and that one should turn one's self to God: Think about God that day and not about work – you have six days to do that. However, what is "work"? If work is what we do during the week, we do not consider what we do on the weekend to be work because we are not paid for it. What is deemed permissible as work on Sunday and not permissible: emergency versus routine work, or continuous work dictated by industry that cannot be stopped, like attending to an electric plant or serving as a nurse in a hospital[45]? We thus tend to construct the meaning of "day of rest" using our own subjective interpretations, except in areas that are legislated by the blue laws. A rest day means a pleasure day for some. Others get exhausted from too much domestic work on that day of rest. We literally turn the concept upside down and dissociate it from its fundamental religious meaning as set forth in the Old Testament.

As a consequence of the permeability of these boundaries, one may speak of intersecting or overlapping temporalities as individuals participate in both the Christian Sunday and the civil Sunday. The dominant civil calendar, which is not a totally independent or secular calendar because it is heavily influenced by the Christian calendar, serves as an umbrella covering the Christian, Jewish, and Muslim calendars in the United States. Each one of these religious calendars has its own rhythms marked by liturgical or communal devotional times and its own logic regarding worship practices. Even when these calendars coincide with the secular state calendar, the meanings may differ. For example, for the state, Sunday is instituted as a day of rest, while for Christians, it is foremost a day of worship and then of rest. Furthermore, the state's definition of a day of rest is less restrictive than the church's definition. Because of the Christian influence on the civil calendar, the secular calendar accommodates Christians better than worshipers of other faiths. In the United States there are ethnic calendars that intersect, but do not coincide with the

Gregorian calendar, and the state is distancing itself more and more from Christian religious influences by repealing Sunday legislation and by refusing to police the Lord's Day on behalf of the Christian majority.[46] This allows people to work as they please, as in the case of California since the turn of the century.

The blue laws as a system of practice

Policing these permeable boundaries thus is a problematic activity fraught with contradictions and difficulties. Although the maintenance of the blue laws depends on the support of the local community, they are not enforced or implemented without causing pain to some and objections from others. Part of this problem may be related to the imagined or perceived collusion between the blue laws and the Christian practice of worshipping on Sunday. Their implementation has been to the disadvantage of some groups including Jews, Christian Sabbatarians, and a segment of the business community. In addition, policing the boundaries of the civil week as defined by the blue laws results in racialized conflicts because the temporal arrangement places the European majority in a temporal position superior to that of the subaltern others, including both Jews and Muslims. This conflict comes about by controlling the developmental pattern of the week.

While the blue laws succeed somewhat in projecting a civil identity for the civil Sunday, as we have seen, they are couched in a religious language borrowed from the Jews and the Christians. Thus the use of the concept of "Sabbath breaking" in the blue laws to refer to the violation of such prohibitions (art 2 sec 3).

Sabbath violation is not a secular concept, and its violations are not a violation of civil law, but rather a violation of religious law. Imposing fines and jail terms for what is a religious violation confuses the civil purpose of the law.[47] The use of this religious concept also blurs the spirit of the law.

Blue laws imply an intervention by the state to prevent the undertaking of work activities during a specific day of the week. It is not any day of the week, but a day already identified in western Christendom as the Lord's Day, a congregational day, a day of worship and a day of rest.[48] These laws thus reflect the policies and practices of the Christian majority. As in any democracy, the majority makes the rules. To the extent that the selection of Sunday as a national day of rest was influenced by religion, the legal principle of the separation of state and church is not upheld in this specific arena, nor is it based on the common interest and will of the community. The Constitution guarantees the protection of free assembly such as attendance at a synagogue or mosque on the Sabbath day and the practice of any kind of religion. Enforcement of the blue laws on the Christian majority thus is disciplinary, while enforcement on the non-Christian group is a form of subjugation.

What interests us here, however, is not a history of the blue laws as a way of enforcing the Christian practice of worshipping on Sunday, or even an explanation of the circumstances under which the blue laws have been abolished or trimmed back. Instead, the focus is on people's reactions to such laws and the ramifications of the blue laws in their daily life.

Jews experience the blue laws as discrimination and resent them accordingly. In 1976, New York repealed its restrictions on Sunday shopping while it maintained its ban on liquor sales on Sunday.[49] For Jewish businesses, the liquor laws instituted in 1934, which prevent liquor stores from opening on Sunday, are more than an inconvenience. They literally lead to loss of revenues. Unable to sell on Saturday because of the Sabbath obligations, Jewish merchants are not able to sell on Sunday, either. This loss of revenues ostracizes them more than the mainstream Christian businesses, which are free to open on Saturday. These laws are seen by many in this quarter as penalties imposed on Jews by the Gentiles or Christian majority. As a Hasidic Jew, the owner of a kosher liquor store, bluntly states: "I cannot serve my neighborhood . . . They are penalizing the Jewish community. Ask anyone."[50] This sentiment was echoed by Rabbi Aaron Pearl of Temple Beth Rishom: "If some people don't want to shop on Sundays, they certainly don't have to, but don't tell me I can't open my store or shop on Sunday because of your day of rest."[51]

The inconveniences that these laws cause for secular mainstream individuals likewise are resented, especially when Christmas, New Year, or Passover eve falls on a Monday. People are unable to purchase liquors on the eve of their holy days or holidays. Commiserating over the fact that his constituents cannot access liquor stores on Sundays that precede Christmas and New Year's Day, Assemblyman Pat Casale states that "this past year was one of those years in the liquor industry when this happened . . . This year, people took for granted they could buy their wine and liquor the day before and they were left dry. It ruined many people's holiday meals . . . and backed up the whole industry."[52] Assemblyman Jack McEneny astutely summarizes the sentiments of his constituency when he refers to their inability to purchase beer between 3:00 a.m. and noon on Sunday: "Try leaving for a picnic at Grafton when you are leaving at 11:00 in the morning and want to pick up a few items in the grocery store . . . What it tends to do is not [so much to] deter people from drinking, but [to] inconvenience families during picnic season. Give me a break."[53]

When people cross borders into areas under the regime of the blue laws, inevitable transgressions result. The following story of a man who was fined ten dollars for fixing his car on Sunday while visiting his daughter expresses well the inconveniences of the blue laws when they are too strictly applied.

> I had just pulled to the curb when I noticed a green puddle of antifreeze coming from under my truck . . . I looked underneath and saw it was my lower radiator hose, but when I took the hose off with a screwdriver and clamp, this officer pulls up to me and rolls his window down . . . He said "you know I can give you a summons and have your truck towed away for working on your vehicle today?" I told him, look, I'm all dressed up, I don't want to be fixing this, but it'll be ten minutes and I am going to fix that hose, so you do what you have to do.[54]

A few days later he received in the mail the summons for a ten-dollar fine. Unwilling to comply because he was attending with an emergency situation, he went to court, pleaded his innocence, was found guilty for working on Sunday, and disappointedly and grudgingly paid the fine.

Finally, the blue laws promote such border crossing to escape the inconveniences they occasion. When a contiguous county or city has blue laws and its neighbor does not, people drive out of town on Sunday to do their shopping where it is permitted. Such a circumstance allows competitors to benefit from this extra sale. For example, it was found in the car dealership business at Danbury, Connecticut, that "potential business was being siphoned over the border into New York, where car dealers are open on Sundays."[55]

In short, if Sunday is a day of rest, those who for whatever reason do not worship on Sunday must adjust to the dominant week, losing money and taking a day off against their will. Over time, this discriminatory condition brings a lot of resentment. This situation also better positions the dominant group, since every thing rotates around Sunday: class schedules, business, transportation, rest day, and worship.

This is not a costless enterprise, since it results in added revenue for one group and the loss of revenue for the other. It is constructed to benefit and accommodate the dominant group. This discrimination is specific, and not general, since it affects certain groups (observant Muslims and Jews) and not Christian Caribbean immigrants, for example.

The transglobalization of local temporalities

With European colonial expansion and the imposition of Western time in the colonial possessions, as we have seen, the Western temporal infrastructure was globally established. The imposition of the civil week that regulates the schedule of institutions that dominate the world and that upholds Sunday as a day of rest therefore is now a global reality. The global status of civil Sunday emerges from two different directional processes: globalization by colonization and modernization, a state project, and globalization by diasporization, an individual project. In the former, it is the expansion of the West in the Rest, while in the latter, it is the presence through immigration of the Rest in the West. Thus, there is a dichotomy in the way in which the global Sunday is effected. In its top-down manifestation, it is imposed by the state, while in its bottom-up version, people activate the globality of the day by going to church and through transnational communication with overseas friends and relatives.[56]

The blue laws of New York thus in fact provide only a local coloration to a global practice that is endowed with new meanings in the context of Western modernity. The relations of civil with Christian Sunday in New York City are a local outcome of a global process that began in Europe in 321. They have their roots in and have been internally shaped by this European tradition. The local performance of civil Sunday cannot be meaningfully understood outside this global context. The civil Sunday as a global day attains a universal status and manifests its local face in different shapes. In the United States, it competes with the Christian Sunday for hegemony, while in other parts of the world, it is a day of rest distinct from the day of worship of the majority, or not a day of rest at all.

Both the civil and Christian Sunday thus function in the United States not just as diasporic temporalities, but as nodes of a transglobal temporal apparatus. The United States does not have a national Sunday that is temporally identical in every state. There are several different Sundays, from the Eastern Time Zone to Alaska and Hawaii. It is Sunday in New York before it is Sunday in California. And there are different Sabbath laws in different states. An American in New York may work at a time when someone is not able to work legally in Alabama.

Because of the prominence of the West in international affairs, its civil week dominates all the other calendars in matters related to commercial transactions and political practices. With the closing of the banks, financial markets, and Wall Street, the globality of the civil Sunday is now a universal phenomenon. The civil Sunday is able to impose itself throughout the world in a way that the Christian Sunday has not.

Yet the Christian Sunday is inherently transglobal. The transglobalization of the Christian Sunday can be described in terms of its constitutive elements: its emergence from Europe, its content as it anchors itself for its meaning on the resurrection of Jesus, its spread through diasporization, and its globalization through its multiple linkages and networks of interconnectedness that constitute the Christian community as a universal body. The unity, diversity, and globality of Christians is manifest through the practice of worship on Sunday.[57]

The transglobalization of Christian Sunday can further be seen in two ways in that it refers to two different realities or practices. On the one hand, it refers to the interconnection of the Christian faithful through the use of a specific day of worship in the week when they externalize their faith in the same divine reality. On the other hand, it refers to a cosmic conceptualization of time shared by the transglobal Christian community. Here, transglobal time converts localized space into transglobal space or links different local sites to each other. The Christian Sunday in reference to eternity is the incarnation of "endless time."[58]

One may speak of a multiplicity of globalities in reference to different temporal religious practices. For Christians throughout the world, Sunday is a global or cosmic temporal institution: As brothers and sisters, they are in communion with each other and stop whatever they are doing to commemorate the resurrection of Jesus. This we may refer to, after Robertson, as "the interpenetration of the universalization of particularism and the particularization of universalism."[59] A specific group of people located in various sites throughout the world are doing the same thing and are connected to the same entity – God as revealed through Jesus. This Christian globality has its boundaries, content, forms of expression, and space. We think that it is different from the boundaries of other globalities. The same can be said of Jews and Muslims. On Friday, Muslims are globally connected to each other in this expression of their faith. Jewish globality does not coincide with Muslim globality, geographically speaking, and the latter does not coincide with the globality of Christianity in terms of space covered.

When we take into consideration the perspective of the actor-participant, we think that it is more accurate to speak in terms of multiple globalities, because the same person may participate in more than one globality and also because the contour of a particular globality may change over time. For example, the global Christian Sunday is longer than just 24 hours because it starts at different times throughout the globe depending on one's time zone and because it may be Sunday here and Saturday or Monday elsewhere. This global reconceptualization of the day of congregational worship poses a new challenge for observant Jews, in particular, because the new global boundaries of such a day must be taken into consideration in order not to desecrate someone's Sabbath. In the following chapter, we explain how Jews have carved a niche for their own weekly cycle in reaction to the civil week and in interaction with the Christian week.

3
The Jewish Chronopolis and "Temporal Identity" Politics

Social temporality is the time that difference makes. By means of it, diasporized ethnic communities experience the difference that time makes. The social temporalities of ethnic communities are diasporized because these immigrants establish themselves outside the confines of their homeland. A diasporic week thus is a temporal outpost of the homeland that is linked to it, directly through transnational relations, symbolically through the uniformity of religious practices undertaken on Sabbath day and during holy days, or both. In New York City, the Jewish weekly cycle is diasporic because it did not originate there, but came into being as a result of the immigration of the population into the United States. This temporal identity is not homogeneous because of the diverse background of the Jewish population (Israeli, European, Mediterranean, Middle Eastern, Latin American, and so on), because of ideological divisions within the population (secular Jews versus Orthodox, Reform or Conservative Jews), and because of the diversity within these categories. Nevertheless, in spite of or because of this diversity, Jewish identity in New York is a node in transglobal networks that connects that local expression to other diasporic sites and to Israel. Transnationality rhythms the cadence of its expression through the High Holidays that constitute important moments of its performance, days and festivals when the community becomes aware of its difference. These times demarcate the community from the rest of society and relink it to its homeland, separating sacred time from secular time, Jewish time from Gentile time, the Jewish calendar from the Gregorian calendar, and the life cycle of observant Jews from the life cycles of others. They define the Jews of New York as citizens of a chronopolis.

The Jewish Sabbath is separated from the days of work in the Jewish week, marked by appropriate rituals and by a period of transition or day of preparation to observe the Sabbath. In New York, Caroline Katz Mount recalled, "Friday nights and Saturdays were set apart from the rest of the week. My father gave up his work clothes and dressed up in a suit, a white shirt, and a tie. My mother did not write or smoke."[1] The Jewish Sabbath is the most restrictive of all the weekly holy days celebrated by the three monotheistic religions, Judaism, Christianity, and Islam.[2] In the United States, the difference between the Jewish Sabbath and the overlapping Christian and civic weeks affects all sectors of public Jewish life, eliciting responses that range from compromises and adjustments, to protests, to the ghettoization of private life and the creation of a temporal enclave.

In the past, to cite one example of how this difference operated, for mainstream society in the United States, Saturday was the time when primary state or local elections were held and examinations for civil service jobs were administered.[3] Because these coincided with the Sabbath, observant Jews were left outside the political process and could not compete with Gentiles for government jobs. To hold elections on Saturday was a not so subtle way to prevent Jews from voting, and this temporal form of discrimination was sometimes engineered from above to neutralize the Jewish vote in state elections. Thus, "when Louisiana's legislature resolved to hold primary elections on Saturdays, a united Jewish community, viewing the measure as somehow more discriminatory than Sunday laws, urged a veto by the governor."[4] In a multitude of such ways, the temporal divide between the Jewish Sabbath and the structure of the civil and Christian weeks emphasized the parallel juxtaposition of the two temporal cycles and sustains the hegemony of mainstream time.

The shift from Saturday to Sunday as a working day likewise refracted on Jewish social life in mainstream America. As Glazer reported, "when Sunday comes, it is embarrassing to have the children playing outside while the Christian children go to Sunday school and church."[5] This becomes a burning issue in the suburbs when children who attend the same schools and play together during the week are prevented from joining the other children on the Jewish

Sabbath. Observant Jewish high-school students are not able to partake in recreational activities with their peers on Saturday – as members of football teams, for example. Even when they want to participate in such games, they still have to deal with the objections of their parents. According to one of my informants in New York, "some kids do not join these sport teams because they would have to play on Saturdays. I mean I know kids who play soccer, like [Ruth's] family. However, they don't join a team. She did not want them to play soccer because all the games and practices are on Saturdays." Similarly, "orthodox College students, because of the time they must give to daily prayers and Sabbath observance, participate less in campus social life and extracurricular activities."[6]

Inevitably, observant Jews have had to develop ways to accommodate the disjunction in their social lives between the Jewish week and the structure of the civil and Christian week. In particular, Jewish Americans in places like New York could not remain immune to the structure of the Christian Sunday as enforced by the blue laws, as well as by the pervasive influence on all aspects of social life exerted by the Christian and civil weeks. Jewish Sunday schools are one manifestation of this influence. We are told that "the earliest Jewish Sunday schools in the United States were started in Philadelphia . . . in direct and deliberate imitation of Protestant Sunday schools."[7]

The clear conflict between the civil week, with Sunday as a day of rest and Saturday as a working day, and the Jewish week, with Saturday as the Sabbath, also has required that Jews develop ways to minimize the consequent economic effects of the difference. Because "the business life of the nation [is] adjusted to a Christian calendar,"[8] but Jews are not able to transact business on Saturday, the heaviest business day of the week, they have developed niche markets on Sunday that they alone control, especially for groceries, in places where blue laws prevent Christians from opening their shops. This strictly Jewish market day provides a needed service to the community in search of household necessities.

To prevent bankruptcy of their economic operations, many American Jews have opted to use Saturday as a working day, thereby being unable to partake in the orthodox Sabbath even if they are inclined to do so. Many also work on Saturday in order to keep their employment, as they did in earlier times, when the six-day week was the norm.[9] Because of Sabbath restrictions, throughout the nineteenth century, while mainstream Americans worked six days a week, observant Jews were forced to work only five, thereby involuntarily enjoying a two-day rest period. As Sarna and Dalin[10] put it, "On Saturday they rested to uphold the demands of the Lord and on Sunday they rested to uphold the demands of the state."[11]

The determination of observant Jews not to work during the Sabbath was held against them in matters of employment. To solve this issue, Jews sought employment and employers that did not require them to work on Saturday. We are told that "immigrants were attracted by jobs . . . [that] could provide . . . the opportunity to observe the Sabbath."[12] Sometimes Jews sought out Jewish employers in the hope that that would solve their religious conflict. But seeking employment from another Jew could be a handicap. As Stiles[13] puts it, "many Jewish employers themselves will not employ their own co-religionists, but give preference to non-Jews because of the economic necessity of keeping their business going on Saturday." The Sabbath has even interfered with the rights of the unemployed. We are told that "Jews . . . were denied unemployment benefits in different cities when they refused to accept jobs involving work on Saturdays."[14]

In addition to forsaking the Sabbath for the sake of economic gains, Jews have taken other steps to alleviate the burden of their temporal dilemma. Since the nineteenth century, Reform Judaism has adjusted the time of the Sabbath service to allow more participation from the working class. Several schemes were developed to do so. Reform Judaism moved the Sabbath service as needed from its Saturday morning niche to Friday evening, Saturday afternoon, or even Sunday, as supplementary to the regular service or as the only service.[15] As Sorin puts it, in some cases, "late Sabbath afternoon services [were held] to accommodate those forced to work in the earlier part of the day."[16] In several cases, as happened at the Immanuel Temple in San Francisco, the synagogue returned to the traditional Saturday services when it became possible to do so, while in other cases, the move became a permanent feature of the congregation.[17]

Because of the economic penalties that follow from the difference between the hegemonic and subalternized temporalities, the practice of the Jewish Sabbath in mainstream US culture has required flexibility, as in the case of those who work in the hotel industry. The following, although extreme by some standards, shows the extremes to which Jews have had to go in running businesses that cannot be closed on Saturday because of the kinds of services they provide:

> The owners of Grossinger's, the famous kosher hotel in the Catskills, are not supposed to do business on the Sabbath; yet clearly it would be impossible to close down the hotel and send away the guests every weekend. So every Friday night before sundown Jennie Grossinger "sells" the hotel to one of her gentile employees for the sum of one dollar – and every Saturday night after sundown she buys it back again.[18]

In all these instances, we see how Jewish temporal identity in the diasporic situation of the United States and New York City is expressed in the context of mixed time – in the interaction between Jewish time and the time of the Christian and civil week. These interactions are not choreographed in an isolated niche. The expression of this temporal identity is structured by the relations between hegemonic and subalternized diasporic temporalities.

Temporal identity politics

To put it another way, as these examples show, the discussion of Jewish temporality carried out here is not in the postmodern frame of reference that sees identity as being fragmented, fractured, malleable, fluid, and multiple, with an emphasis on the subject position. Neither is it our intention to attempt to define Jewish identity as self-production or self-fashioning. Instead, we view it as a result of interactions with mainstream society.

Identity seen thus is inherently political, and "identity politics" is inherent in the very nature of diasporic communities and hegemonic and subalternized groups.[19] When we speak of "identity politics," we do not mean a body of specific issues, but a general set of processes – interaction, boundary maintenance, and conflict – through which identity is shaped in interaction with other groups.[20] The Jewish week has developed its subaltern identity in New York because of the subaltern position of the group in relation to the Anglo-American community. In this framework, "temporal identity politics" means the struggle of the subalternized group to maintain its different time structure, to overcome the subalternity of its temporality, and to develop temporally harmonious relations with the rest of society. As we have seen, the temporal identity politics of Jewish New Yorkers is itself performed in a number of ways. These can be decoded to unveil the dynamics of its parameters and the characteristics that reflect its social texture.

The numerous recurring controversies over the Christmas tree in front of city hall, the holiday on Good Friday, and daily school prayers or religious instruction in the classroom are symptoms of struggles over temporal identity politics. The ultimate goal is the dominance of the hegemonic group over others by co-opting the state to support, recognize, and legislate that dominance. It is a quarrel over time: the identification of the hegemonic, public and civil time with a religion and the subalternization of other times. The time of the secular state is used to facilitate, if not to consolidate the temporality of a specific religious ideology. The consolidation of the Christian week of the majority with the hegemonic civil week necessarily means the minoritization and subalternization of the others. As Sarna and Dalin[21] note, "Children of minority religious groups ... must either subject themselves to being singled out as non-conformists ... subject themselves to the pain of not belonging ... or they must participate in religious practices and teachings at variance with what they learn at home or in their religious schools."[22]

The negotiation of identity in situations such as these often requires a movement back and forth between the ways of the subalternized group and the ways of the state. While employed in civil society, for example, the Orthodox Jew escapes at certain moments from the itinerary of the day to return to the high moments of the religious day. The beginning and end of the Jewish day do not coincide with the beginning and end of the civil day. Instead, the Jewish day generally runs in parallel with the civil day, crisscrosses it frequently, but does not coincide with it. These intersections are sites where the subalternization of Jewish temporalities is enforced and experienced and where that subalternization is submitted to, negotiated with, and resisted. When one faith is identified with the state, the others are subalternized and it is in these relationships that they interact, grow, develop, and reproduce.

Diasporization as subalternization

Diasporization implies subalternization because, as the temporal dilemmas encountered by Jews in New York City that we have examined illustrate, an immigrant group enters a social system that is already stratified by ethnicity, social class, and religion. In some cases, the diaspora locates itself at the upper echelon of society, but in most cases, it enters the social system through its bottom stratum.[23] It is subalternized. The location of the group in the societal system reflects both its locality and its ensuing globality. The group becomes the nexus where both the global and the local meet and the site where globality has a local face and locality a global face.

Diasporic subalternity may occur through different processes because of the different positions of the diaspora in society. It is important to identify the type of subalternization that we are referring to here so as to distinguish the Jewish case from other companion cases. Some diasporas become subalternized as a result of structural changes in society that can lead to downward mobility from a dominant societal position. This is best exemplified in the case of the Spanish settlers after the US occupation and later independence of the Philippines. Other diasporas, such as Native Americans in the United States, are subalternized because of colonization, which subjected them to a position of subjugation. Some other diasporas become subalternized because of racial or religious discriminatory practices in their new land, as in the case of Muslim immigrants from the Gulf states. Still other diasporas are subalternized because of their religious or linguistic practices, and not because of their race. This is the case of European Jewish immigrants. While some form their own linguistic ghettos in New York City and are subalternized only in this aspect of everyday life, others form religious ghettos, enclaves that require the ghettoization of critical aspects of their temporalities to sustain their religious life. Diasporization in such enclaves entails the subalternization of "community time."

Community time is a concept that heralds the temporal identity of the group, that provides a temporal infrastructure that ties the members to each other, that contrasts their time with other temporalities, mainstream and subaltern, and that provides the temporal framework of reference for the relations of the group with outsiders. As Graham and Graham note, "the notion of 'community time' embodies the idea that community relationships are patterned over time, and that involvement in these relationships is not simply a matter of individual choice. Community time is marked most explicitly by infrequent symbolic rituals, but it is also acknowledged in the rhythms of everyday interaction between community members."[24] The concept of community time dissociates time from space. That is, it is not a prerequisite for the community to be located in a specific place or locale. Such a community is defined by the cultural temporality that symbolizes membership and a sense of belonging to the group.

The "community week" – an extension of community time – refers to the deployment of the week according to a logic that is intrinsic to the cultural practices of the group. Such a structure emanates from the homeland and, with diasporization, intersects with the mainstream week. Diasporization implies spatial expansion of the homeland week, and in some cases, the multilocal expression of that week. As a consequence of the multilocality of its manifestation, it implies transnationalization and transglobalization as the mechanisms that provide the infrastructure for its sustenance, reproduction, and adaptation. Acceptance of the identity of the community week in one place can be used to further its acceptance in another locale. Such an action is premised on the understanding that the community week is a tentacle of a homeland temporal structure and maintains its identity because of that connection. The week is thus a local temporal manifestation of a global temporal phenomenon.

The genealogical formation of the subalternity of the Jewish Sabbath

While diasporization may explain the globalization of the Jewish Sabbath, it may not necessarily explain its subalternity *vis-à-vis* any socially constructed hegemonic religion. This is so because not all diasporized religions are subalternized. For example, as we have seen, Christianity has established its hegemony in the Western world through diasporization. In fact, through the first century of the Christian era, there was no hegemonic religion in the Roman Empire that commanded the attention of the vast majority of subjects. Judaism, Christianity, and other faiths were struggling for survival as they attempted to open religious spaces so as to express their religious beliefs without interference from without. During this early period, the institution of the Sabbath was hegemonic among both Jews and Christians precisely because the leadership and the rank and file of the early Christian church were both Sabbath-worshipping Jews.[25]

Therefore the subalternity of the Jewish weekly cycle in New York cannot be explained by an exclusive focus on contemporary practices. Such an explanation must be sought in the events that earlier separated Christianity from Judaism and that also hegemonized one while subalternizing the other. To be brief, the subalternity of the Jewish Sabbath, and by extension that of the weekly cycle it embodies, began shortly after the death of Jesus, not before, because Jesus himself observed the Jewish Sabbath. To understand the context in which Western Christianity imposed itself as a hegemonic faith on both Eastern Christianity and Judaism, one must invoke three occurrences: the conflict for hegemony between the "church of Rome" (Roman Catholicism) and the "church of Jerusalem" (Eastern Orthodoxy), which led to the separation, the different organizations, and the different traditions of these two Catholic churches; the will to de-Judaize Christianity as manifested in the actions and writings of the Church Fathers, who intended to provide the primitive church with a distinct identity; and the tradition of holding a "church service" or, more precisely, an informal gathering, on Sunday in memory of the resurrection of Jesus and thereby encouraging Christian Jews to shift their allegiance from the practice of Sabbath to the Sunday prayer meeting.[26] At first, this Sunday service was not meant to replace the Sabbath, but to add a Christian dimension to it. However, in order to prevent any type of confusion in the minds of new adherents, to hide away from Roman anti-Semitism, and to consolidate the identity of the faith, the observation of the Jewish Sabbath was eventually discontinued by the Christian faithful.

The era of Constantine was fundamental in the separation of Judaism from Christianity because until then there were Christian Jews who routinely continued to practice Judaism. But in 321, when Constantine established the *dies solis* (Sun day) as a day of rest, the identity of Sunday was also established as the hegemonic day of the week, giving preference to and accommodating the Christians at the expense of the Jews. This official act of the emperor accomplished five things simultaneously.

First, it propelled the globalization of Christianity, because from now on, the empire would identify with a structure of the week that was more suitable to the Christians than to the Jews by giving preference to Sunday instead of Saturday as a day of rest. The available historical evidence seems to indicate that, initially, the emperor did not necessarily make that connection to accommodate any one group. Rather, the situation was exploited by the Christians to advance their religious cause. In any case, this change in the calendrical structure of the empire worked to the advantage of the Christians at the expense of the Jews and contributed to the regional expansion and later hegemonization of the faith.

Simultaneously, it propelled the globalization of time by forcing everyone in the empire to observe the same day of rest, and, in the process, it gave an official imprimatur to the structure of the week. The seven-day weekly cycle with a Sunday peak day became the temporal rhythm that cadenced the social temporalities of all the inhabitants of the empire. From then on, all of the other days were considered work days and thus shared an identity distinct from that of Sunday.

At the same time, it propelled the marginalization of the Jewish Sabbath through its subalternization *vis-à-vis* the Lord's Day. In 321, the Jewish religion, week structure, and day of rest and worship were officially subalternized with the official identification of Sunday as the rest day throughout the empire.

The act of the emperor also instituted the civil week as modeled on the Christian week, with Sunday as the day of rest. Thus, 321 became the official birthday of the establishment and globalization of the civil week as we know it today. Until then, the seven-day cycle was more an ethnic and religious temporality than a civic one. With the Act of Constantine, the Christian seven-day cycle became civic temporality, as well.

Finally, having led Judaism to a position of subalternity and marginality, the Act of Constantine subjected Jews to a general condition of exclusion that they could not change when they later migrated to other corners of Western Europe, Eastern Europe, and eventually to the United States. This later migration structurally located them in a minoritized position in the United States. The origin of Jewish exclusion as a system of temporal practice in much of American history thus can be traced back to the era of Constantine.

The minoritization of the Jewish week thus was a European product before it was an American, or before such subalternity became Americanized. Subalternity has its genealogy, and in this case, it hybridizes the global network of Jewish temporalities. Some nodes are hegemonic, as in the case of Israel, and others subalternized, as in the case of the Jewish weekly cycle in New York City. Since the colonial era there, the Christian majority has sought to transform the identity enforced by the dominant civil week into a hegemonic Christian identity and in the process to subalternize, co-opt, trivialize, or ignore the religious and cultural identity of the other weekly cycles.

In New York, not only have the blue laws helped the rapprochement between Christian Sunday and civil Sunday, as we have seen, but by placing the Jewish week in a subaltern position, they have forced Jews in New York to develop a number of different strategies – strategies involving crossing or defending the boundaries between Jewish and non-Jewish identity as experienced in the clash of temporalities between the Jewish week and the civil and Christian weeks.

Deminoritizing the Sabbath: Inward change

The Sunday blue laws were passed to protect Sunday, the majority's day of worship, to prevent Jews and others from desecrating the day, to subalternize the Jewish Sabbath, and to proclaim Sunday as the peak day of the Christians. These were not neutral, but discriminatory laws whose intent was to colonize and subalternize Jewish temporal practices, and at times even criminalize them.

Hegemonic practices tended to elicit the Balkanization of the reactions of the subaltern because of their different class positions, ideological leanings, and pragmatic considerations. Some Jews objected to the blue laws on the principle of state–church collusion in reference to the First Amendment of the Constitution, while others had no objection, provided that they were exempt and allowed to work and attend to their commerce on Sunday, since their day of rest was on another day. Still others felt that this was majority rule and all should abide by the blue laws.[27]

In the long run, however, any subaltern group is likely to work toward its deminoritization. Minoritized groups utilize diverse strategies to deminoritize themselves. Assimilation is sometimes used for this outcome. Other times, resistance strategies are developed to make claims on the majority. In other words, the group may proceed with inward change to adjust itself to the majority or may push for outward change so that its needs can be met. The choice and relative success of these two strategies for the deminoritization of the Jewish week has depended on the size and political influence of the Jewish population. In areas where they were in small numbers, they could not easily resist the hegemony of the Christian week cycle and tended toward strategies of inward change – basically, strategies of assimilation. However, in places where the population was demographically important, their enclave had the strength to maintain their own weekly cycle and to work for its legitimation via change in the mainstream society. In his ethnography of neighborhood Jewish life, Kaplan has found that "in those very large centers where they may comprise an important part of the merchant clan [they] maintain their own work rhythm in the week. In Opelousas they had to adjust to the general system or lose out in the competitive race."[28]

Temporality is an important factor for understanding inward change. This is in opposition to other legitimate practices of assimilation, such as conversion (joining a dominant congregation at the expense of one's faith), interethnic marriage (exogamy), and deghettoization (sociogeographical dispersion). Time is identified in this frame of reference as a criterion in the production of inequality. Saturday worship has always placed American Jews at a disadvantage with the majority society, which takes its day of rest on Sunday. They are also at a disadvantage in areas where blue laws are still enforced, which prevent them from engaging freely in all kinds of business without cause for concern.

When religion is a factor of minoritization, instead of race, language, and culture, there are fewer avenues open for such a change short of transforming the theological content or ritual practices of one's faith. Inward change implies the implosion of some aspects of that faith. The Sabbath was identified as the principal locus for transformation in order for the group to articulate its time with the temporality of the mainstream.[29] Temporal deminoritizing via inward change therefore has meant transferring the Sabbath from Saturday to Sunday to coincide with the majority day of rest. The relocation of Sabbath day in the weekly cycle was perceived as a possible solution to the Jewish American dilemma in their attempt to mesh with the larger public. It was a way to use Jewishness to express Americanness.

The location of the Sabbath on Saturday helped minoritize twice as many observant Jews in New York in terms of practice (the religion of a nonhegemonic group) and time (located on the busiest market day in the West). Relocating it on a different day, as Reform Judaism did, deminoritized it in terms of time, but not in terms of religion. Such a temporal relocation reduces the temporal conflict with the mainstream by making one available for work on Saturday, which is a working day for the mainstream.

Such a relocation of the Sabbath does not collapse the majoritized and minoritized week, but rather synchronizes them, with each keeping its own identity. In effect, this strategy turns the Jewish American week into an American week while keeping its distinctness as Jewish by means of a double calendar: the Jewish calendar for the High Holidays and festivals, and the Gregorian calendar for the routine of everyday life. This attempt at synchronization is often done at the expense of the Jewish calendar, however, as youngsters become less familiar with the complexity of its time-reckoning system, immersed as they are in the Western solar calendar.

Of course, the major reason behind this move was to accommodate the requirements of the work week as set forth by the majority and the dominant temporal system. The transfer of the Sabbath day in this new regime followed specific syntactical rules of the religious landscape: Relocate the morning Sabbath service inside the Sabbath day (from Friday sundown to Saturday sundown), but at a different time, (Friday evening or late Saturday afternoon, for example), or relocate it outside the boundaries of the Jewish Sabbath day, that is, on Sunday (from Saturday sundown to Sunday sundown). While in the first example a theological justification is not needed because the service is still observed on the day of the Sabbath, in the second, there is a rupture between the practice and the theological rationale that is supposed to sustain it. By transferring the Sabbath from Saturday to Sunday to accommodate hegemonic temporalities, the theological foundation for the seventh day (story of the creation in the Book of Genesis) cannot be transferred to the first day. A new theological justification was needed to explain this day, just as the Christians did when they adopted Sunday in memory of the resurrection of Jesus as the day of worship for their emerging sect. In the case of the Christians, the shift was to put the emphasis not on the theology of the creation of the world by God, but rather on the theology of the resurrection of Jesus, the first day of the week or the day following the Sabbath.

The effort of Reform Judaism in juggling the day of Sabbath was to find a way to deminoritize the temporal life of the group and to preserve their religious practices in a way that nevertheless articulated the temporal expression of their faith with mainstream time. But this inward change is just one aspect of the struggle of their diasporic time with mainstream time. Another aspect is the effort to effect outward changes by making claims on the majority society so that the subaltern temporality can be expressed side by side with mainstream temporality in a legally recognized, democratic space.

Deminoritizing the Sabbath: Outward change

The alternative to assimilating the minitorized Sabbath to the dominant day of worship and rest by inward change was to gain recognition of the legitimacy of the minitorized Sabbath itself. Such an opportunity was not simply offered to Jews who adopted this strategy. They had to establish their democratic rights as a religious group to determine their own temporalities. They then had to extend those rights, sustain them against counterclaims based on the right of the majority to set a day of rest for all and to prohibit certain activities contrary to the purpose of the day as a way of nurturing civic citizenship and promoting the common good, and they had to make the observance of those rights part of the routine practices of civil society.

The acquisition of temporal rights is necessary not simply because it targets an issue that is winnable, but also because it is an issue on which the group may be unwilling to negotiate a different outcome. If such a right can be attained, it will serve as a bedrock upon which the group can acquire additional rights.

The crusade of the Union of Orthodox Jewish Congregations under the leadership of Henry Pereira Mendes focused on just such an issue. In 1898, military authorities had already requested to allow Jewish soldiers and officers time off on Saturday and the High Holy Days so that they might fulfill their religious obligations. Since the army was intent on keeping order, allowing two different days for Sabbath, one

for the Christian soldiers and the other for the Jewish military personnel, was not a small request. While this could, perhaps, be granted
previously in specific cases, now it was extended to the entire army
as a new way of doing business. Instructed by President Theodore
Roosevelt, the War Department developed such a policy, allowing
Jews to attend services on the Sabbath and Jewish holidays.[30]

The way temporal rights are accumulated depends on an "ice-
breaker" that makes possible a cascading effect whereby the right in
question is extended to other areas of life and other rights are recognized, as well. Once a right is legitimized in one area, it is possible to implement it elsewhere and to ask for more. The right to a
Saturday Sabbath was being violated in several different spheres of
public life, such as the educational system, the business sector, and
the government. Once the right to a different Sabbath was acquired
in the military, the same arguments in its favor could be used in these
sectors. In addition, it could be argued that what makes sense to
the military should make sense throughout civil society. Victory in
the military thus opened wide the gates for redress elsewhere.

The Union of Orthodox Jewish Congregations was able to gain the
transfer of "bar examination from the Sabbath," to obtain "Sabbath
privileges for Jewish students at City College," and to receive "leaves
of absence for municipal employees on Jewish holidays."[31]

The acquisition of rights often involves the contestation of those
rights by the majority because their own rights may often be
infringed upon, as in the case of employers who must let employees
go to synagogue services. Sustaining temporal rights once they are
acquired means struggling not to lose the ground under assault. This
can lead either to the routinization or the extinction of such rights.

Temporal rights become integrated into the routine practices of the
society when the legitimacy of the acquisition of these rights by
the group is no longer questioned by the majority. These rights
now become part of the routine of daily life.

The day of preparation

While Judaism has dealt with the minoritization of the Sabbath in
New York City and its subaltern status there by both inward change
and by acquiring temporal rights that alter its outward status in
society, the ways in which it has tried to deal with the status of the

so-called "day of preparation"[32] and the problems that arise from observing it have been more complicated, and some of those strategies have been less successful. The task was to find a way to insert the day of preparation, with its unique, subalternized temporalities, inside a dominant social formation that already had its own temporal rhythms.

Friday has always been a day of material and spiritual preparation for the Jewish Sabbath. The day of preparation and the Sabbath form a continuing temporal segment: The existence of the former depends on the existence of the latter. There would not be a day of preparation without the Sabbath. In the nineteenth century, when Reform Judaism moved the Sabbath away from its natural niche to Sunday, for example, the day of preparation had to be moved, as well, to adjust to this newly manufactured, reconstituted, and diasporized Jewish weekly cycle. The day of preparation is affected whenever the faithful decide to move the day of worship to another location in the weekly cycle.

The day of preparation is unique because it is the only day whose identity is ambiguous. It partakes of the working week because it is a working day, and it partakes of the Sabbath because of the spiritual preparation it entails. Hence, it is transitional in character. Because of its betwixt-and-between position, it is a liminal day, with all the ambiguity and hybridity that presupposes. The day of preparation is tied to the Sabbath, and, in this sense, it is different from the informal and formal preparation for the Sabbath among Christians and Muslims. The day of preparation is specific to Judaism. Since Friday is not a day of rest in Islam, there is no tradition of a day of preparation there. Instead, Thursday evening (which for the Muslims is Friday evening) is a time when the faithful prepare themselves, along with Friday morning for the midday *Juma'a* prayers. The preparation for the Muslims thus does not start on the day before, but on the day of the congregational prayer, since the preparation on Thursday evening and Friday morning is part of the same Muslim Friday. The Catholic Church never had a formal day of preparation, and cooking or cleaning on Sunday, for example, is not forbidden by canon law. Catholic confession, which used to occur on Saturday for those who had transgressed God's commandments, can now take place on Sunday and is not required, as it was before the Second Vatican Council.

A rabbi provided the theological explanation of the day of preparation:

> The day of preparation can be understood only in the context of the metaphor that says: "One who toils prior to Sabbath merits to eat on Sabbath." So what does it mean? In this world our toil is to plant the seeds in God's garden, metaphorically speaking. One who toils to plow the field and plant the seeds, to work on themselves in this world, to work on their heart, and their own temple, one who works during the week merits to eat on Sabbath, merits the reward of eternal life. What is the reward of eternal life? Basically, we were put here to be godly, to the extent that we are godly, that we evolved from being barbarians, that we have evolved to become godly, this is the extent of our accomplishment in this world, and that's the preparation of the great Sabbath. And so the preparation is a very necessary part, a prescription of Sabbath; it is to prepare specifically for Sabbath.

Unlike the Sabbath, whose contours are ritualized, the day of preparation is theologically unstructured, simply a time during which the faithful are supposed to make themselves ready to enter the Sabbath, both materially, in terms of food preparation, the cleaning of the house and of one's clothes, and also spiritually, in terms of the disposition of the heart. The day of preparation thus is a day that people are free to fracture it as they please, as long as the conditions that specify its identity are met. There is no uniform way of partaking in the day of preparation. Each household develops its own tradition. The rabbi further remarks:

> The preparation may start any time on Thursday evening, and sometimes it seems that people start cooking on Thursday evening, because they don't have time on Friday. So it does involve a host of chores. So there is spiritual and material preparation. In a Jewish family you often see, children, everybody, pitching in to help. There was a show done by the Endowment for the Arts many years ago, I think it was called *Remnant of a Holy Nation*. It was trying to make the parallel between eternal life and the preparation that we do in this world, and the actual preparations for the Sabbath and the great feast. Making sure that all the beds and spreads are all cleaned and fluffed.

A middle-aged Jewish New Yorker – Deana – recalls how the day of preparation was handled by her mother when she was of school age in the 1960s and describes the temporal boundaries that separate the day of preparation from the Sabbath:

> My father did not come earlier on Friday. Both my father and my mother had to work, and my father could not get off early. But somehow she managed to prepare us this extra meal for Friday night, and I don't remember how she did it. Maybe she did come home a little earlier on Friday. But, she always cleaned the house on Thursday. She was always someone who prepared things ahead, and so one of the things I do remember her doing was leaving notes for us on the table – when you come home from school, turn on the oven, put the roast beef in – you know – turn it up to this temperature. It is possible she left earlier on Friday.
>
> Okay. We were more traditional than religious, and my mother did things the way her mother did them. Her mother was born in Romania and came to the United States at the turn of the century. So it was kind of her version. She would prepare a special meal, usually chicken or roast beef, something really big and special, and she prepared it all afternoon. Before we had dinner, she would take this candleholder, put it on the top of the refrigerator, light the candles, kind of cover her head with a cloth and cover her eyes with her hands, and say a special prayer, but she did not include us in it, and then we would have dinner. Then, from the time she lit the candle on Friday night at sundown, there were certain things we could not do. We could not write, color, cut with scissors, or sew.

Because this day begins the night before, much of the food preparation is carried out on what we refer to as Thursday evening in the Gregorian calendar. One woman remembers what her mother did in preparation for the Sabbath: "On Thursday nights, she would work particularly hard, preparing for the Sabbath. She would bake her *khales* [braided Sabbath loaves], roast the goose, cook fish, make noodles, and prepare the compote."[33] I also learned from informal conversations with Jewish New Yorkers that on Thursday evening, Orthodox families cook and clean. In some households, the wife does not go to work on Friday so that she may prepare the home for the

Sabbath. One informant spoke of his mother and grandmother, who carried out this tradition in his family, and said that now his wife does the same.

The material and spiritual requirements of the day of preparation, however one chooses to fulfill them, have definite social and economic effects that underline its subaltern status as a temporal formation. The day of preparation interferes with business in two ways: It is the day when observant Jews buy things for the Sabbath and also the shortest business day of the week, since the number of hours stores are open is reduced to allow the faithful enough time to return home for the opening of the Sabbath. As a business day, Friday is different from the other days. The day of preparation intervenes in the workplace, not because the orthodox Jewish worker fails to show up, but simply because he may shorten his presence at work in order to take time to prepare for the Sabbath, which may fall before 5:00 p.m. in the winter. During the winter, some leave the place of employment before the regular end of the work day so that they will not desecrate the Sabbath.[34] Golden[35] notes that "their livelihood had to permit them to go home before sundown on Friday to prepare to observe the Sabbath on Saturday and go to work, if possible on Sunday. Obviously they could do this conveniently as entrepreneurs, self-employed. So they became manufacturers and peddlers, or contractors for manufacturers, or they worked for other Jews."

Employees sometimes lose money because of the time lost at work. And society as a whole is affected when businesses must close earlier than usual because of the Sabbath. It is well known that in Manhattan, such Jewish establishments as the jewelry stores are not always open late on Friday afternoon. An Anglo informant told me that in addition, it is difficult to attend Orthodox Jewish photo shops because the pressure is on to do business as quickly as possible, if the stores are open at all after 3:00 p.m. store owners are in a mood to get ready for the Sabbath. While the proprietors of Jewish stores thus are well aware of the need of their employees to take time off, Gentile store owners sometimes need to be reminded of that. It is reported, in one case, that "the demand was made that work be stopped earlier on Friday afternoons so that the Sabbath might not be desecrated."[36] In firms where the workers are allowed to telecommute or to use flextime, however, Friday does not constitute a time-management problem.

In July 1999, I interviewed Jewish merchants and store owners on two Friday afternoons in the Diamond District on Forty-sixth and Forty-seventh Streets between Fifth and Seventh Avenues in Manhattan, and I observed the gradual closing of their stores before the Sabbath. I was told that during the winter, they close their stores about 1:00 p.m., and during the summer, they close around 3:00 p.m. because of the difference in the beginning of the Sabbath and the ability to reach home on time. The reason that they close a couple of hours before the Sabbath is to ensure that even if the subway is behind schedule, it will not interfere with the opening of the Sabbath. Not every merchant had a substitute to replace him for the remaining hours. However, those who had Gentile partners just left the operations to them.

Temporal substitution

One strategy that observant Jews employ to deal with the social and economic effects of subalternized status of the liminal day of preparation is temporal substitution. They substitute work hours that are unambiguously outside both the day of preparation and the Sabbath for hours that might conflict with those temporalities, replacing time involved in Jewish religious observances that conflicts with the time of the civil week with time that does not.

The fact that employers cannot count on observant Jews to remain at work until closing time on Friday, depending on the season and the time of the opening of the Sabbath, sometimes creates problems between management and workers. The employer may not want to let the employee go before 5:00 p.m. How is such a problem solved? I asked a working-class Jewish American, who said:

> The problems don't always get solved. Usually the way that they are solved is if the person puts in overtime, or extra hours. They'll have them stay late one or two nights a week, or if the firm is open on Sunday, he'll be on the Sunday shift, as well. I used to work half days on Sundays to make up for the half days that I was not working on Fridays.

Some Jewish workers also come in early on Friday to replace the hours in the afternoon during which they are not able to work.

Temporal substitution also is carried out for the purpose of circumventing the law of the Sabbath that forbids work on that day. Since Gentiles are not covered by the covenant of the people of Israel with Yahweh, they are not forbidden to work on Sabbath, and therefore substituting their labor in times when a Jew is prohibited from working is permissible. Thus, as we have seen, one can benefit from the work of a Gentile who replaces oneself in carrying on activities that are prohibited to Jews during the Sabbath. Colin L. Powell, the secretary of state during the George W. Bush administration, recalls that while growing up as a teenager in New York City, "on Friday nights I earned a quarter by turning the lights on and off at the Orthodox Synagogue, so that the worshipers could observe the Sabbath ban on activity."[37]

Temporal substitution is an official recognition by the Jews of the parallel complementarity of Gentile temporality. When an observant Jew substitutes his own hours of labor in the civic or Gentile regime of temporality for hours in the day of preparation, Gentile temporality is constructed as hegemonic, and Jewish temporality remains minoritized. But when an observant Jew substitutes the hours of a Gentile's labor for hours in the day of preparation, it is Gentile temporality that is constructed as subsidiary, something to be used for the sake of keeping the Sabbath holy. In that construction, there is a temporal inversion in the stratification of times. The time of hegemony (civil time) becomes subservient time, and subaltern time (Jewish time) becomes hegemonic.[38]

Temporal substitution implies that the replacement is undertaken to allow the person to observe the holy day, that the replacement is limited in time – one day or more (Sabbath and Jewish holy days), that it is a requirement of a faith (Judaism), that the believer returns to his routine day life at the end of the sacred period and that both the Jew and the Gentile see it as a transitional event.

Temporal substitution allows for more flexibility at the workplace and cooperation among people of different faiths, and, by micromanaging work time, it provides a ready-made solution for potential disruptions of the workplace. Golden[39] speaks of a condition that "leads many Orthodox Jewish families to have a Gentile as their servant, so that they can drink the tea and warm themselves by the fire, made by him, without technically violating the law."

It is worth mentioning two variations in the practice of this form of temporal substitution among observant Jewish Americans in New York City. In a situation where a booth was rented for the weekend so as to participate in a sale show, a Jewish merchant showed his wares on Friday, and since he did not have a Christian partner to replace him at the sale show on Saturday, he simply left his cards and pamphlets on a table in his rented booth on the Sabbath, hoping that anyone who did not observe the Sabbath would pick them up and call back later. On Sunday, he returned to the show to take care of business. With this strategy, he observed the Sabbath, and in order not to waste a day of work on Saturday, he substituted the actions of his potential customers for his own labor.

The other variation we have already noted: that employed by a Jewish hotel owner who used to sign a contract every Friday ceding the ownership of the hotel to a Christian partner, then regained the ownership of his property after the Sabbath. It is usually more convenient for Jewish business operators to have partners who are not Jewish, because then they can technically arrange the books in such a way that the ownership and the profitability of the Sabbath goes to the non-Jewish shareholders.

Temporal substitution thus is the site or crossroads where two times meet. It implies the coexistence of two moral orders. It is the reverse of proselytizing, in which where one encourages another to convert. Here conversion is not an issue, since, whether it is from the subaltern or the hegemonic point of view, the recognition of justified alterity is the cornerstone that makes that transition possible. Temporal substitution implies the recognition of different temporalities with different logics, the maintenance of these temporal boundaries, the intersection of these temporalities without mixing, the exploitation of one by the other for religious purposes, and the play of subalternization and the hegemony in a system constituted by their difference.

Hybrid temporality, or mixed time

In addition to temporal substitution, another strategy that observant Jews employ to deal with the social and economic effects of their subalternized status is the hybridizing of temporalities in the deployment of the Orthodox Jewish practices. By "hybrid temporality" we mean the mingling of different times, sometimes via acculturation, syncretism, interpenetration, or simply via assimilation because of the incorporation of the Jewish week inside the civil week.[40] In addition to being a strategy of assimilation, however, hybrid temporality can also be seen in terms of multicultural resistance, as Jews employ it as a strategy to maintain the distinctness of their temporality in the face of structural constraints from the dominant sector of society.

Hybrid time thus appears in different forms. One can think, for example, of the assimilationist mixing of ritual times as Reformed Jews moved the Sabbath from its Saturday niche to Sunday or the forbidden mixing of ritual time with secular time, which can be considered as a form of transgression, as when the Sabbath is said to be desecrated because one accomplishes impermissible activities during such a day. However, the strategy of hybrid temporality also appears in the permissible, nonassimilationist mixing of secular time with ritual time, as happens in the "*eruv* of cooking," or the expansion of secular time inside ritual time, as happens with the "*eruv* of the private domain."

An *eruv* is a mechanism used to circumscribe and circumvent rabbinical law (not Torah-mandated law) for the purpose of doing secular activities on the Sabbath. According to Jacobs,[41] an *eruv* is "a legal device by means of which two areas or periods are mixed or combined in order to provide a relaxation of the Sabbath and festival laws." This definition refers to the internal dynamics of the community and indicates quite clearly that such a device affects both space and time and is the mixing of space and time. More often than not, the spatial reference is emphasized at the expense of the temporal dimension of the phenomenon. This is particularly true when the matter is brought to the attention of the courts.

In *Joseph M. Smith et al. v. Community Board no. 14 et al.*, the Supreme Court of the State of New York provided a relational definition of the *eruv* in an attempt to decide whether the existence of such a device constitutes an infringement on the establishment clause of the First Amendment of the United States Constitution. For the court,

> an eruv, under Jewish law, is an unbroken physical delineation of an area. In tangible terms, it is created from natural barriers or

from wires strung across poles. Among other things, an eruv must be built on land owned by the public, it may not have a ceiling, it must be at least forty inches high, and must be accessible to the public twenty-four hours a day. This device allows an observant Jewish person on the Sabbath to carry or push objects from his residence, i.e. private property, onto public property and vice versa, activities such as a person would be prohibited from doing otherwise by creating the fiction of a communal "private" domain. Although its use is specifically for the Sabbath, the eruv is maintained throughout the year by observant Jews. New York has about thirty existing eruvs, there are nine eruvs in New Jersey, and many others scattered throughout the United States.[42]

An *eruv* may be erected for the purpose of symbolically joining two or more houses and yards in order to transform them into a single domain, thereby allowing one to carry things from one house to another or from the house to the yard – a behavior that is not allowed on the Sabbath. As the United States District Court for the District of New Jersey has opined, "under Jewish law the eruv does not alter the religious observance of the Sabbath, it merely allows observant Jews to engage in secular activities on the Sabbath."[43] Wigoder notes that "in many neighborhoods and cities, especially in North America, an eruv is erected, often utilizing telephone poles for this purpose."[44]

The *eruv* expands the religious space to include secular space, and in the process changes the identity of the latter.[45] The conversion of space leads to the conversion of time as time enters the picture through spatial expansion. Once secular space becomes part of the religious domain, it also enters a different temporality: It moves from civil time to Jewish time. The expansion of space by means of the *eruv* thus also is the expansion of time, as well. The regime of the civil and Christian Sabbath is the opposite to that of the *eruv*: It reduces the religious space, and by extension the spatiality of religious time, by allowing a Gentile at home to carry out inside this private domain things that the observant Jew is not allowed to do. The civil and Christian regime is not so much a mixing as a juxtaposition of temporalities along the dividing line between public and private domains.

For a Jewish family living in an American city, the construction of an *eruv* helps solve practical problems in the practice of the Sabbath.

These concerns are spelled out in a concise fashion by Linda Boroff, who notes that:

> the main advantage is that it [the *eruv*] enables Orthodox women to bring young children to synagogue or to take them outside their own property. Without an eruv, Orthodox Jews are prohibited from carrying a child outside the home or pushing a child in a stroller on Sabbath . . . In addition, observant Jews cannot carry prayerbooks, keys, combs, umbrellas or even canes or crutches when they leave the house on the Sabbath.[46]

The *eruv* "for cooking" or of "prepared foods" is another example where civil time is expanded inside Jewish time and allows the observant Jew to circumvent the rabbinical law concerning work on the Sabbath:

> When a festival falls on a Friday, it is forbidden by rabbinical law to cook on the festival for the immediately following Sabbath, even though cooking on the festival for the festival itself is permitted. If, however, a person has already begun cooking on a weekday before the festival for the Sabbath, he may continue, as it were, to cook on the festival for the Sabbath. By making an eruv . . . the food cooked before the festival allows one to "mix" the cooking done on the festival for both festival and Sabbath needs.[47]

There are thus different types of *eruv*, all of which accomplish this hybridization of temporalities in one way or another: the "*eruv* of courtyards," the "*eruv* of domains", the "*eruv* for cooking" and the "*eruv* of boundaries."[48]

Only one type of *eruvim* has come to the attention of the Gentile New Yorkers because of the controversy that surrounds its existence: the *eruv* of private domains. In April 1, 1985 four Orthodox congregations completed the erection of an *eruv* in Belle Harbor, New York City, which "span[s] Beach 16th Street to Beach 149th Street and the beach to Beach Channel Drive, an area covering approximately ninety blocks, use[s] sixty-three New York City lamp poles, [and] increase[s] the height of sea fences covering ten city streets to a minimum of forty inches."[49] The erection of this *eruv* was challenged by a resident of the area on the basis that it violates the establishment clause of the First Amendment of the US Constitution. In the affidavit that he deposed with the court, Joseph Smith, the plaintiff, argued that "the only way to avoid this unwelcome and unwanted religious device and the resultant religious aura and metaphysical impact in the area would be to move away from the area and find residence elsewhere."[50] In the view of the court, no such violation of the First Amendment had occurred.

Redrawing the boundaries of ethnic space may require entrenchment over majoritized space or the conversion of aspects of the latter to complete the reorganization of the former. Therefore, the symbolic ethnic space institutionalized through the erection of an *eruv* brings forth its own logic inside the larger domain of minoritized space, and since the expansion is engineered by the diasporic group, and not the majority community, it is likely to raise two sets of conflictual issues: between the adherents of this new arrangement (observant Jews) and the larger diasporic group (non-Orthodox Jews), and between the minorities and the majority.

The objections against the construction of *eruvim* in American and other Western cities are leveled mostly by Jewish neighbors for the specific reason that they do not want to be encircled by observant Jews whose presence would remind them of a faith they no longer practice. They also object to the likelihood that such an *eruv* will attract other Orthodox Jews to the neighborhood, which may transform their quarter into a Jewish ghetto and eventually expose the community to anti-Semitic attacks. Many anticipate that such a transformation may increase the cost of renting or buying housing in the neighborhood and may lead to the eviction of long-term renters on fixed income. Finally, some believe that the existence of an *eruv* in the neighborhood might compromise "city sovereignty over public domain" and constitute an "erosion of private property rights and the improper use of the city's police power."[51] All of these arguments were presented to the courts in a handful of states, and the courts never upheld them, which explains the existence of *eruvim* in such cities as New York, Washington DC, Seattle, and Los Angeles. Instead, observant Jews have successfully employed the hybridization of temporalities to achieve the theologically permissible, nonassimilationist mixing of secular time with ritual time. They have in effect created a temporal enclave that is one expression of a broader phenomenon – a transglobalized chronopolis.

The globalization of the Sabbath

We have been focusing on the diasporized temporalities of the Jewish week in the United States, and in New York City, in particular. Jewish temporal identity is a historicized and socially constructed production through which Jews express and cadence their daily lives. However, these local temporalities are also global, and no analysis is complete without paying attention to the expression of that communal temporality via the global processes linking identity to transnationality and globality,[52] analyzing the location of Jewish temporal identity in the double process of flows and closure that is characteristic of globalization and elucidating the particular characteristics of this community as a chronopolis.[53]

As a consequence of the diasporization of the Jewish people throughout the ages and throughout the world, the population became transnationally interconnected through family links, business networks, religious institutions, formal voluntary organizations, and informal grassroots relations. The result has been the globalization of the Jewish week and Sabbath. This chronopolization has produced a distinct temporality, with the Saturday Sabbath a distinct "global day" in the Jewish weekly cycle. On that day, the faithful everywhere around the globe reconnect spiritually with Israel – the mystical center that makes the crisscrossing and border-crossing transnational linkage possible.

The Jewish Sabbath came to the United States through Europe by way of microglobalization. The same laws that prevented Jews from hegemonic ascendance in Europe were implemented in the United States for the same purpose. This new diasporic niche constituted a node in a global network of Jewish settlements. It is a global spiritual phenomenon. With the celebration of the Sabbath, the Jews are united with the state of Israel throughout the Diaspora. In the *Union Prayer Book*, one reads, "Blessed be the Sabbath, the queen of days, which brings unto Israel enrichment of soul. Even as Israel has kept the Sabbath, so the Sabbath has kept Israel."[54] Through the Sabbath, the Jews are in communion with each other wherever they live. It is a distinct public expression of a global diasporic practice.

Globalization is not be understood here as homogeneity, but rather as producing heterogeneity. Local Sabbath practices reflect historical conditions, cultural contexts, and modes of incorporation into the dominant system. For Biale, "The Jews were arguably one of the first and most successful global people. Jewish merchants in the Mediterranean and in Northern Europe created global networks long before the Internet. Yet, this global culture, linked by the Hebrew language and by a common legal system, also developed its own local customs and character."[55] However, the use of the Internet changes the parameters for how we understand the Sabbath because it casts new light on the globalization of this institution. One may speak of the global stretching of the Sabbath through Internet use in contrast to its local stretching through the *eruv* system. To have a sense of the problem, I asked a Orthodox rabbi who operates an Internet company to comment on the expansion of the Sabbath in terms of the spatiality of global time and the temporality of global space:

> There's a whole question about how the [rabbinical] law is interpreted for Internet companies. I've heard a number of different opinions on it, actually. But one thing that is pretty much agreed is that during the period of time that it is Sabbath for the person that owns that company, his company should be sold or closed. There's actually been a suggestion that for the period of time that it is the Sabbath anywhere in the world, a Jewish-owned company should post on its website that "It's Sabbath in your area; we are not available for business."
>
> If you live here in San Francisco, you are forced to follow the Sabbath according to California time. Should we have a global Sabbath? It can only be local, because it is only according to the movements of the sun, and the earth in relation to the sun, so it can only be local. The *revvi* once said to behold from the heavens the little girls and the mothers lighting the candles all around the globe for a sweep every week, around the globe for twenty-four hours.
>
> But at the end of the Sabbath here is the beginning of the Sabbath somewhere else, so one seems to be getting inside of the other. The question is then: Am I responsible for ensuring that I do not do business in a place where it is Sabbath? Or am I responsible only to not do business when it's Sabbath for me? There may be an answer, but what I've heard is that it is a question that is gray. Because the question is, if the market is not a Jewish market, it's just Sabbath for me. However, if they're Jewish

people, even if they are ignorant of the Jewish laws and customs or estranged for other reasons, then I am participating in their desecration of the Sabbath. And do I want that on my head? Would I rather teach them that this is Sabbath rather than taking money from them on this day, which, according to the Torah, would be a sin to exchange money on Sabbath, now what am I doing? I'm facilitating a sin.

So specifically, we've been looking at a time clock on some of our Internet companies that will come up with a little non-interactive cartoon, that once you're there you can watch the cartoon, but you can't maneuver in it. It will teach you that it is Sabbath, and it will teach you the whole philosophy of why we have closed down all the interactivity for that time period. We should really give the non-Jewish people codes so they can get in, but that is discriminatory. We would never hear the end of it. I see all of those inconveniences of it.

I don't know if there is a Torah obligation, any kind of strict enforceable obligation to the Torah to discontinue commerce over the Internet to a place where it is Sabbath there. Certainly there is a directive to discontinue business in the place where the person owns the business, where the person lives. But the dilemma, where it gets gray, as I told you, is more of an issue of a stumbling block before the blind. If I am being an opportunist at my brother's expense, even if he doesn't perceive it that way, but I perceive it that way, then would I, in fairness to my brother, want to do that? That is why we have concluded we are going to be putting a time clock on our interactivities on the Internet, so that we will share with people that it is Sabbath in their locale during that period of time and explain to them why we are not providing interactivity for twenty-four hours.

What we do, what we ended up doing when I was in Israel working with companies in the US, was to send US businesses a calendar that gave them the exact times that I would be available and when I would not be available. I told them up front that as inconvenient as this may be, that this is based on the banks not being on strike. Once you include the banks and the postal workers on strike, we would be lucky to get a few days a month of actual interaction. Again, it is like the telecommuting stuff is good, and the Internet is quite good. A person on his Friday will send his message out and then on Saturday after the Sabbath the guy will turn on his computer and be back to work and he has all the stuff sitting there. It's doable, it's all quite doable.

The study of the ways in which the use of the Internet interferes with Sabbath practices in other time zones is still in an embryonic stage precisely because no specific rabbinical law has been issued to provide guidance on this question. The virtual reality of cyberspace links locales to each other and thereby establishes a global infrastructure for interconnectedness and interaction.

The notion of the global Sabbath that characterizes the chronopolis in which the Jews of New York participate belongs to the category of particularistic universalism that characterizes diasporic globalization. It is a practice that expresses the religious faith of a group and that does not coincide with other diasporas' practices in terms of content, sites covered, weekly rhythms, and people involved. The global Sabbath materializes itself through the agency of local sites that are the strategic nodes that make its translocalization possible. Other nodes, other practices, are linked to other transglobalized sites in the chronopolis inhabited by New York's Muslims, as we will now see.

4

The Muslim Chronopolis and Diasporic Temporality

Two observations can be made concerning the social integration of the Muslim week into mainstream civil time by the Muslims in New York City, irrespective of these diasporic citizens' country of birth.[1] On the one hand, Muslim immigrants engage in social practices that are regulated by civil society and that follow the rhythms of the civil week. They thus inhabit a diasporized Muslim temporality that has been Americanized. At the same time, however, they also inhabit a temporal enclave or chronopolis that links them to worldwide Islam via an Islamic calendar that gives direction to their daily, weekly, and annual activities. These two sets of social temporalities often intersect and crisscross each other, which makes it important to analyze the Muslim week in American society if we are to understand the mechanisms of the constitution and transglobalization of the American Muslim chronopolis.[2]

The Muslim week as practiced in the country of origin undergoes a transformation that adjusts it to the constraints of the workplace in New York, the regulations of the state, and the conventional rhythms of the civil week. But the Muslim week also affords the basis for a locally distinct globalized temporal identity that is characterized by the cultural content of its global flows, the direction and spatiality of its transnational networks, and the temporal rhythms that cadence these flows. The nature of these double identities will be examined here in terms of their internal restructuring and their external relations with the rest of society. Here again, as in our study of the Jewish week in New York, and throughout, our concern is with the nature of the interactions of the subalternized temporality with hegemonic mainstream temporalities.

Muslim immigrants are an even less homogeneous group than Jewish immigrants. They come from distinct cultural and national backgrounds as diverse as Iran, Egypt, India, Morocco, Turkey, Lebanon, Pakistan, and Syria.[3] While some immigrants have lived in a Muslim state where the Islamic calendar is hegemonic (for example, Iran or Saudi Arabia) and diasporization constitutes their first adaptation to a civil or Western calendar, others, such as Turkish immigrants, have adapted to this adjustment in their country of origin prior to immigration into the United States. Even in this latter case, they were accommodated at home by the public and private sectors so as to be able to engage freely in their weekly Friday communal prayers. In contrast, the municipal government and the business community in New York City have yet to come up with ways of accommodating the different temporal deployment of the immigrant Muslim week. In this sense, for both groups of Islamic practitioners, their adjustment to the West is a novel experience that has challenging constraints unknown to them before their emigration from their homeland.

In this study of the Muslim week in New York, the focus is exclusively on the immigrant population from the Persian Gulf states, and not on Caribbean, African, or Afro-American Muslims. Since African-American Muslims or members of the "Nation of Islam" hold their religious services on Sunday, we will not deal with the temporal rhythms of their weekly activities. This study concerns itself with Gulf states' immigrants precisely because of the traditional emphasis they place on Friday congregational prayers. In some of these countries, such as Saudi Arabia, Friday is the official day of rest of the civil population. However, in other Muslim states, such as Turkey, Sunday has become the official day of rest as a result of external pressures to readjust or replace their national calendar with the hegemonic Gregorian calendar of the West because of international trade requirements and interstate relations.[4] Even though, for some, Sunday is designated in their homeland as a day of rest, Friday continues to play a predominant role in their secular weekly activities because of the Koranic injunction to attend the noon prayers at a mosque on that day. Observing this injunction retroactively affects the flow of business practices during the week.

The Islamic week is distinguished from other weeks not simply by its distinct peak day – Friday – but also because it forms a distinct

"temporal domain." By its rhythm, cadence, and mode of organization, the Islamic week contains the basic characteristics that organize
daily life. As Zerubavel puts it, "through imposing a rhythmic 'beat'
on a vast array of major activities (including work, consumption, and
socializing), the week promotes the structuredness and orderliness of
human life, making it more regular and thus more predictable."[5]

We saw in the study of the Jewish week in New York a diaspora
engaged in a series of negotiations with the temporalities of the
mainstream culture over temporal identities, employing a series of
strategies adapted to the particular subaltern identities involved. In
the Muslim diaspora, we encounter a different set of such negotiations, with strategies adapted to different identities – to different
forms of assimilation and also to the production of a different kind
of enclave, ghettoized or dispersed, that has a cultural rhythm on a
par with that of the original homelands and that thus constitutes a
different kind of transglobalized chronopolis, a global city with its
own distinct temporal orientation. This latter strategy may disrupt
the temporal harmony of mainstream society by inserting its temporality in the fabric of the social system. This practice implies that
the diaspora establishes its temporality as a guidepost for the cultural
life of the group, as a barometer to measure and judge its adaptations
to city life, as a collection of strategies used to bend city ways in areas
in which the immigrant group is unwilling to compromise, and as
an infrastructure for the American Muslim chronopolis.

The analysis of the Muslim day and week thus calls for both an
interpretation of their reconstitution in New York City and an examination of how the temporality unique to this group fractures the
geometry of the urban social system. These analyses will be carried
out through an examination of the temporal niche expressed in the
physical landscape the Muslims occupy in this immigrant and mod-
ernist city. To understand that, we must examine the place of Friday,
the peak day, in the structure of the Islamic week, and also the nature
of the Islamic day as I observed them at a makeshift mosque in mid-
Manhattan.

When I arrived at the mosque, there were about three hundred
people in the basement of this modern office building, attending
the Friday congregational prayers. This group of Muslims had been
renting this basement since 1991 for between $3000 and $5,000 per
month. The basement is the only spot they occupy in the building.

The rest of the space in the building is occupied by law firms and other professional offices.

New York Muslims do not come to the mosque for all the prayers. They recite some while at work. At the workplace, they lay their carpets in some corner, sometimes in public view, sometimes in their offices, to pray facing east. At first, co-workers find the practice strange, but as time goes by, they adjust to it. So Muslim workers have brought a new religious dimension to secular Manhattan. Like the Orthodox Jews before them, they have carved a niche for the performance of their daily rituals.

On this Friday, Muslims were assembled in the main hall of the basement, in the small office of the imam, in the corridors, and on the steps leading to the exit door on the first floor. The basement was packed with worshippers. Some who could not get in at all were praying in front of the building on the sidewalk. Those outside the building laid their carpets, took off their shoes, faced east, and performed their prostrations and prayers. Some passersby, perhaps tourists, were amused at seeing them praying so publicly without being disturbed by onlookers.

While in some areas one national group or another dominates by their numbers in attendance, in most urban mosques, the congregation is rather diversified. It was found in New York City that "most of the city's mosques attract an amalgam of regular congregants, shopkeepers from the local neighborhood, or perhaps a few cab drivers in the vicinity during *Juma'a*."[6] Diversity certainly characterized this Manhattan mosque. I was told that on a weekly average, about eight hundred people come to this mosque for daily prayers and meditation, mostly individuals who work nearby and taxi drivers. Every day they come from all walks of life: street vendors, mostly from West Africa, operators of food carts, mostly from Egypt, Pakistani and Bangladeshi office workers, cab drivers from everywhere, who complain about the difficulty of finding a place to park their vehicles, Indonesian immigrants, overseas Chinese, Albanians, North Africans, and students from Turkey. I spoke at length with the imam (an Egyptian American), an elder (a Turkish American), and an attendant (from West Africa) who works at the *New York Times*.

My impression was that in terms of social class, the membership of the congregation was mixed, from the bourgeois to poor daily workers, but once they were in the basement with their shoes off, it was difficult to distinguish them by class. It was notable, however, that there was only one woman in attendance (an African American woman), who was confined to the office of the imam. Gender separation, gender exclusion, and gender marginalization transpire through the strengths of the male membership.

Friday and the structure of the Islamic week

For the Muslim faithful, the Islamic week indirectly derives from an act of "divine revelation" for the Prophet Muhammad that directs them to use Friday as a congregational day of prayer.[7] The Koran is strict about this prescription and presents it as an obligation to the faithful. Verses 9 to 11 from chapter 62 provide the social context and religious meaning of the peak day of the Islamic week.[8]

> 9. O you who believe, when the call is sounded for prayer on Friday, hasten to the remembrance of Allah and leave off traffic. That is better for you, if you know.
> 10. But when the prayer is ended, disperse abroad in the land and seek of Allah's grace, and remember Allah much, that you may be successful.
> 11. And when they see merchandise or sport, they break away to it, and leave thee standing. Say: what is Allah is better than sport and merchandise. And Allah is the Best of Providers.

The exegesis of verses 9 and 11 reveals or implies that the day of congregation is a work day and that Muslims, upon hearing the call for prayer, must leave all their earthly activities – commerce, sport, or any other – and attend the gathering (*Juma'a*) at the mosque. So work is permitted before the congregational prayer. Verse 10 also indicates that after prayer, one may return to work, confident that entrepreneurial activities may be successful because of the grace of Allah. Friday thus is parceled out in three distinct moments according to the Koran: the half-day's work in the morning, the prayer time around noon, and the later half-day's work in the afternoon. It is the only day of the week that is thus fractured.

The centrality of Friday resides in the fact that it is the culmination of the week, when the faithful communicate their joys, sorrows, and intentions to Allah, when they experience fellowship with other fellow believers, and when they are spiritually reenergized for the following week. Hence, the three characteristics of the Friday *Juma'a* can be summarized as congregational prayer, fellowship, and the infusion of spiritual energy for the next weekly cycle.

What distinguishes the Islamic week from the other weeks is that it has no prescribed day of rest. The day of rest in Muslim countries, be it Friday or Sunday, is imposed by the state, and not by Islam. In a sense, the Islamic week is a continuous week, and one weekly cycle touches the other without a day of rest in between the two. In the context of the Islamic week, one is not prevented from earning money on Friday, as happens in the case of the Jewish Sabbath. The justification for working on Friday is from the Koran: "Allah is active every day, He never rests." In my observations in New York, I have found that after the congregational prayer, most Muslim workers indeed return to their jobs.

Friday thus is not even strictly speaking a *day* of worship, but rather a midday worship period in which prayer is proposed for a specific time of the day – around noontime, or in the early hours of the afternoon. However, following Friday prayers, the afternoon is often taken at a slow pace. And while congregational prayer is required of males on Friday, women are not obligated to partake in this ritual.

Although Friday is the most important day for the Muslims, the congregational prayer meeting cannot always be attended on that day by some congregants because of conflict with workplace schedules. The distance of the mosque from the workplace also may hinder one's ability to attend such services. The absence of any nearby congregation of Muslims is sometimes a handicap. This sort of problem concerns the individual in his or her devotional activities, not in adherence to Friday as the peak day of the week. At the Manhattan mosque, I learned that people are likely to attend the mosque near the location they happen to be on the day of congregational prayer – be it at home or at their workplace. This mosque is attended almost exclusively by people who work on Friday in Manhattan. Those who take a day off on Friday, following the customs of their homeland, attend the mosque near their places of residence.

While some Muslims do not adhere strictly to the daily prayers, they may nevertheless attend the Friday prayers at a nearby mosque. The latter have been referred to as the "Muslims of Friday," distinguishing them from the daily practitioners and from the "*Eid* Muslims," who show up for prayers only during the high holy days.[9] According to a Saudi Arabian immigrant:

> Friday is only for those who go to pray. But most people don't, and those who do, [it] is not that they are faithful – it is a tradition that if you pray on Friday, God would hear you more than any other day. *Juma'a* is "Friday" in Arabic and means "group." So people get together on Friday as a group. Friday is like Sunday morning for Christians. You go and pray.

There are several interpretations of the choice of Friday as the Muslim weekly holy day. The first is purely conjectural and refers to the needs for Muslims to worship on a day different from the holy days of the Jews and Christians. Since the Jews have Saturday and the Christians Sunday, this conjecture argues, Friday was selected to give a different and distinct identity to the Islamic faith and its followers.[10] It was an institutional choice to identify, separate, and consolidate one faith from the others by way of de-Judaizing and de-Christianizing it.[11]

The second interpretation is theological and refers to the Islamic narrative of the creation of the world by Allah. In that tradition, Friday becomes a holy day, a day of excellence, because of what Allah undertook on that day. The principal reasons for the holiness of Friday are that, according to Muslims "it was on Friday that Adam was created,"[12] that he entered into Paradise, and that he was sent down to Earth. For these reasons, it is believed that judgment day will occur on Friday. Because of this, congregational prayers are held on Friday, and people are encouraged to give money to charity on this day. As a result of the sanctity of Friday, it is widely believed by the faithful that prayers offered to Allah on that day bear immediate fruit and one's sins are ipso facto forgiven.

The theological explanation of why Friday is not constructed in Islam as a day of rest stems from the fact that Muslims are not asked to subscribe to the belief that Allah got tired after he had created the universe in six days. For Muslims, being tired and in need of rest is the consequence of one's sins, and would imply imperfection and finitude if applied to Allah. This interpretation, according to two Egyptian American imams and one Palestinian American imam I spoke to for clarification on that question, is unacceptable to Muslims.

The third reason is contextual and sociological. According to Goitein, Friday was selected as a holy day in reference to "the instructions given by Muhammad to his representative in Medina to hold the public service on the day when the Jews bought their provisions for their Sabbath."[13] Since Friday was a market day in Medina – the day of preparation for the Jews and a day for restocking merchandise for others – the injunction for Friday prayers implies that the people were already in town, and services should be held before they return home. For Goitein, "the market in Arabia breaks up soon after noon, so that everybody attending it is able to reach his home before nightfall . . . Therefore, the proper time for the public worship was at noon, shortly before people dispersed to get to their homes, and thus it has remained until the present day."[14] This sociological interpretation provides a plausible explanation for both the choice of Friday and the midday prayer.

The "day" in the Muslim calendar

The definition of the day in the Islamic calendar is not the same as in the civil calendar because among Muslims, the day starts at sunset and ends at sunset.[15] The day has a rhythm provided by the five prayers, while the rhythm of the week leads to the peak day – Friday – after which a new weekly cycle begins.

Similarly, the day in the Muslim week is not defined in the same way as the day in the Christian week. The Christian day is not astronomical, but is conventionally based on the rotation of the clock from midnight to midnight. In contrast, as in the case of the Jewish day, the Muslim day goes from sundown to sundown. That is, it comprises a full period of dark and a full period of daylight consecutively. The Christian day contains or covers the second half of the period of dark, a full period of daylight, and the first half of the following period of dark. In practice, the Christian day does not fully coincide with the Muslim day. As Freeman-Grenville[16] notes, "in correct

Arabic . . . the Christian 7 p.m. is 1 o'clock in the evening . . . and what to the Muslim is Sunday evening is to the Christian still Saturday evening." Locating the end of the day at sunset, rather than at midnight, provides a different temporal rhythm that syncopates the life of the Muslim with a different beat than that of the mainstream citizen.

Because Friday is a peak day in the Muslim calendar, the rest of the week tends to rotate around it. Friday separates the week to come from the preceding week in the same way that Sunday does in the Gregorian calendar used by the civil week. The communal prayer mandated by the Koran for that day both spiritually reinvigorates the faithful and is an experience of fellowship. The Muslin turns to Friday as the day of completion, the rendezvous with Allah. This is why the day is considered by the faithful to be "holy."

Although Friday is not a day of rest in some Muslim countries it still shares a number of characteristics with the Jewish Sabbath and the Christian Sunday. It is a day different from the other days of the week because of the obligatory communal worship, the required cleanliness of the body, the purification of the soul, and the fellowship with the faithful. In the external manifestation of the exceptionality and singularity of the day, the clothes that one wears and the food that one eats differ from the routine practices of daily life.

The Americanization of the Islamic week

The Muslim week has not simply been transplanted to the five boroughs. It has been Americanized in several different ways. However, despite its adaptation to urban life in the United States, and although it frequently intersects with the civil week, it does not collide with the civil week and continues to maintain its distinct identity. Studying how the Islamic week is reconstituted in New York will also allow us to identify and explain the mechanisms of operation of this chronopolis there.

The Islamic week is Americanized in three ways: because of the constraints of immigrant life in a non-Islamic state, because of the way Muslim immigrants adjust to the system of the Western week that is heavily influenced by Western European Christianity, and because of the new identity that it forges due to these external factors and the internal urge to conform to traditional Islamic ways.

By "Americanization," we mean that the week contains features of both the homeland week and the American week and is a hybrid product. This is why one cannot speak of it as being a transplantation, but rather as a new production or new creation. Full cultural continuity would have implied structural continuity, which is not the case here.

Instead, the organization of the civil week, with Sunday as a day of rest, influences the structure of the Muslim week. The civil week is not simply a matter of sequence of days, it is also the rhythm of daily life in terms of peak days, the obligation to take Sunday off as a day of rest, and the concentration of leisure activities during the weekend. Immigrant children, for example, must adjust to a different rhythm for the school week. Those who come from Saudi Arabia and Iran, where school is closed on Friday, but open on Sunday, must adjust to the temporal deployment of the American civil week. Children who were not accustomed to going to school on Friday must adjust to a situation in which they have to do so. Those who used to go to school on Sunday must adjust to the fact that Sunday is a rest day during which regular schools are closed. Likewise, the religious education of Muslim children takes place more and more on Sunday as they use the Christian day of rest for Sunday school. In US cities with large Muslim immigrants from the Gulf states, Sunday school has become a main activity at the mosque, irrespective of the immigrants' Shi'ite or Sunni backgrounds. This is one area where the Americanization of the Muslim faith has become most visible.

The fact that secular society stops working on Sunday also forces Muslims to do likewise because non-Muslims are not available on Sunday for business, especially in the morning. The ideology for some Muslims then becomes: Let's worship on Friday and let's rest on Sunday. As one Muslim immigrant businessman put it:

> Yes, most often business merchants will take one day off, and that's possibly Sunday. And there are a combination of reasons: one is if he has children, the children are off school on this day, second, the business is very slow, so they can afford to take the day without losses, and third, most activities, going to the park, taking kids to recreational things, gatherings, Sunday seems to be the day for all of that, so definitely there is a shift.

You could say that the weekend definition that applies to Americans applies to Muslims, as well. There is no difference in many instances.

He conceded that "there are some that do take the day off as Friday" – he mentioned a dentist of his acquaintance – and "some stores also close on Friday, but that's not the majority, that would be the minority. In this area, around the *Masjid* [the mosque], the businesses are open, they close for two hours, and they will attend to the Friday prayers."

"The weekend definition that applies to Americans applies to Muslims" in the structuring of activities other than formal labor – activities as diverse as weddings and the scheduling of academic conferences. As one informant put it,

In traditional Muslim societies, most often Thursday evenings would be the time for the community to gather, like a wedding would occur on Thursday evening, an engagement party, a celebration of a newborn child, any type of community festivity or religious festivity, or any community attempt for gathering, public meetings, usually they would take place on Thursday evenings, and sometimes would go on to Friday evenings. Now in the US, that is completely altered, most of the gatherings that occur in the Muslim community, and here we're talking about the majority of them, are on Saturday evening. Some would occur on Friday evening, and some would occur on Sunday. Conferences, without any exception, would take place on Saturday and Sunday, and some would begin Friday, after Friday prayer, or Friday evening; so they'll begin at seven in the evening and go on to Saturday and Sunday. This is also completely different, because most conferences, let's say in the Muslim world, if they want to start, they'll start on maybe Wednesday evening, if they're two days or more, Wednesday evening, Thursday, and then Friday, with the major gathering being around Friday.

Because of the temporal practices of mainstream society, Sunday rest for Muslims thus simply becomes a practical matter, especially in states where Sunday rest is legislated by blue laws, as in New York. And to the extent that the Christian and secular calendars coincide, the Islamic week reacts and adjusts to the Christian calendars, as well. There are Christian holidays, such as Christmas, that are also secular holidays of the state.

Just as we have seen in the case of the Jewish adaptation to the temporalities enforced by the hegemony of the civil and Christian week, "reform" Muslims have sought to accommodate the temporalities of worship to the temporalities of the mainstream society by moving the day of congregational worship from Friday to Sunday.[17] Such a move solves two problems at once. Sunday is the time when people are free to attend congregational prayer. Using Sunday, instead of Friday, also saves time, since the family may have to come to the mosque to bring the children for Sunday school. Elkholy,[18] who studies the Sunday noon prayer among the Muslim community in Toledo, interprets it as representing "a kind of over-all religious integration with the American environment."

But as with Reform Judaism's shift of the Sabbath, the transfer of the congregational prayers from Friday to Sunday by "reform" Muslims has consequences for the content of the faith itself. Since the belief system underlines the importance of Friday as the day of the birth of Adam, which gives a theological justification to the temporal structure, moving the time of congregational worship from Friday to Sunday disentangles the theological justification from the temporal location that gives it its spiritual and eschatological meaning. The maintenance of the day of worship on Sunday by reformists thus somewhat distances them from traditional Islam and constitutes a major point of theological contention among believers.

However, in general, the shift of congregational worship from Friday to Sunday remains a practical matter, not a theological one: Those who attend the Sunday prayers do so because of their inability to leave the workplace or because they have children they bring to the mosque for Sunday school. Those who are not handicapped by these two constraints, as well as the old or unemployed, attend the Friday service.[19] While in Reform Judaism, Sunday Sabbath replaces the Saturday Sabbath, in the Muslim context, as Haddad puts it, "Sunday services . . . serve only as alternative meetings and do not replace Friday worship."[20] As the study of Muslim worship practices in the Southend found, "Because of the difficulties encountered in leaving work to worship on Fridays, the weekly communal prayer has traditionally been observed only by the elderly and retired men of the Southend . . . The Friday communal prayers . . . almost disappeared as the custom of Sunday worship became the preferred norm."[21]

Research carried out in Quincy, Massachusetts, found that for reasons of convenience, not theology or ideology, attendance of congregational worship on Friday was heavier during the summer months than during the rest of the year, when it was heaviest on Sunday. This was because the faithful came in large numbers on Sunday, when Sunday school was held, to bring their children to school, while during the summer months, when Sunday school was not held, they came in large numbers to the Friday services.[22]

Because Sunday congregational worship is a matter of convenience, not of theology, and because Sunday worship lacks a theological justification, it is easy for worshippers to move back and forth in their devotional practices. They are fervent believers in attending the mosque on Friday, but are ready to shift in order to accommodate themselves and their children. They are simply accommodating themselves to the rhythms of the civil week.

And because the accommodation is practical, not ideological, it can be reversed, just as we have seen a similar accommodation of the Jewish Sabbath to the rhythm of the civil week reversed in a Reformed Jewish congregation in San Francisco. The recent history of the Southend Muslim community, for example, reveals that following the change from the Friday prayer to the Sunday services, worshippers returned to Friday congregational prayers as new settlers reinvigorated the traditional practices of the community: "In recent years, a group of men of varying ages . . . can be found attending the Friday communal prayer. In contrast to the past, this attendance represents a virtual revival of the Friday prayer . . . To a large extent, the revival of the mosque is a direct result of the influx of a large number of new immigrants to the Southend."[23] The new immigrants serve as a catalyst for the reproduction of the transnational relations of the community with the homeland and for the revival of the disappearing old culture in the diasporic neighborhood.

While the disjunction between theology and practical matters means that the Americanization of the Muslim week via "reform" strategies for locating the day of congregational worship is relatively easy and relatively easy to abandon, the conflict between Muslim and civil temporalities in the Americanization of the Islamic weekly cycle is felt more acutely in the deployment of the day itself. Diasporans must attempt to combine and mesh together the features of both the Islamic day and civil day because of the dual religious and secular obligations to which they must attend. The singularity of the Islamic day rests with the scheduling of the five daily prayers. While the morning (*fajr*/dawn) and evening (*maghrib*/sunset and *isha*/night) prayers do not present any problem because they can be done in the privacy of one's home, the daylight prayers, (*zuhr*/noon and *asr*/afternoon) for those who work outside their home, require some adjustment, because they must be done while one is still at the workplace. Indeed, the struggle to accommodate the prayers in the workplace when "there is usually no area at the place of employment where it is appropriate to prepare for and perform them"[24] is the single most important issue that characterizes the adaptation of the Muslims to the civil day.[25] Because of workplace constraints, these prayers are not always fulfilled in the strict order prescribed by traditional Islamic tradition. Instead, their temporal locations are sometimes adjusted to the rhythmic cadence of urban life via prayer clustering.[26] Prayer clustering is a strategy for accommodating religious obligations to the demands of secular social life, a strategy that is permitted under Islamic law. It consists of relocating unsaid prayers to a different moment when they can be combined with the prayer of the hour.

Midday and afternoon prayers have been the best candidates for such clustering. An Iranian woman reflecting on her life in New York, remarks that:

> In the morning and evening, I have no problem to recite my prayers on time. But the only problem I have is with the middle of the day prayers [*zuhr* and *asr*]. We are allowed to combine sets of daily prayers together. I don't know how to explain it. You can ask there is a reason for that. You just pray in the evening, but you say that this is for past prayers. There is a rule for that, but you are not supposed to do that all the time.

Another Iranian American woman interviewed in San Francisco was more casual and less scrupulous about doing the prayers at an exact time. For her, it is an interval of time so as long as you have an idea of what time it is to pray, you know the sun is going down at 5:30, you know you need to get your afternoon prayer done before then. It is better to do it earlier, but it is okay if you do it before sunset. So it is an interval, it is very easy to fit into your life.

Difficulties presented by the sequence of the prayers during the winter months, when sunset falls at an early period, fade away during the summer, and prayer clustering as a way of fulfilling one's religious obligations then is used less often by the faithful.

The temporal location of two of these prayers (*zuhr*/noon and *asr*/afternoon) corresponds to the moment when the practitioner may be at work. The part of the Muslim day that culturally does not correspond to the civil day provides the rhythm for these prayer activities, but at the same time places the Muslim in conflict with the routine flow of work of the civil day. Here, the Muslim is the integrating site where the hybridization of the logics of two different days occurs. There is a back-and-forth motion whereby the Muslim penetrates the secular day for his labor, but reverses on occasion to the Muslim day for devotional purposes. In this new temporal regime, some Muslims thus have developed a flexible identity that is compatible with both the teaching of the Koran and the constraints of daily life in New York. Although from the standpoint of the actor, the secular and Muslim days are not parallel days, but a single integrated day, with prayer times punctuating the routine of daily life in the civil day, what one actually sees here is the deployment of the Muslim day side by side with the deployment of the secular day and their periodic intersection.

Perhaps the best example of the way in which the Muslim week and the civil week proceed in parallel is the way in which the peak day of the Muslim week remains gendered, while the civil week is differently gendered. Gender differences are sustained by a temporal infrastructure, and not simply by a spatial one. Gender is temporized precisely because it is spatialized. Because of the spatial distance that exists between males and females as a result of their different positions in American Muslim society, women occupy different temporalities from men.[27] Muslim gender positioning does not coincide with gender positioning in the hegemonic Anglo community because these two agencies belong to different temporal cycles and proceed from different logics toward different goals.

As we have seen, the Muslim week allocates spheres of public worship in terms of gender by making it mandatory for men – and not for women – to participate in the communal prayer on Friday. This peak day constructs the private realm as the sphere of women and the public mosque as the sphere of men. In relation to mosque attendance on Friday, an Iranian Muslim woman has the following to say:

> Well, for the sisters, it's not as big of an issue as it is for the brothers, because it's not something that they must do, but for the brothers, it is something they need to partake in every week. The women, they are invited to come? Oh, of course, it's best if you do, but it's not necessary. So for the brothers, the few brothers that I know, they just take their lunch-hour break and they manage to come and pray and leave.

The fact that men, but not women are mandated to attend the Friday prayers opens a spatial division that distances each group from the other and reinforces the ideology that confines women to the domestic sphere.

Gender division also is present in the mosque in the physical separation of men and women worshippers, which reflects the different positions that both men and women occupy in society. This division is spatially asymmetrical and reflects spatially that social asymmetry. These gendered practices reinforce and reproduce the gendered ideology that is necessary to justify the asymmetry. The production of these gendered practices is a male project that is part of the effort to reproduce in New York City gendered Islamic identities and ethnicities[28] that devalue diasporic Muslim women and that lead to what Rowbotham calls "women's partial citizenship."[29]

The Muslim woman's social position of course is also asymmetrically temporized *vis-à-vis* the mainstream community because of the minority status of the group. While in the first instance, the inequality factor was the result of different positions of individuals in the same group, here, the disparity is between the majority and the minority communities. These two forms of subjugation are also inscribed in the week. Emancipation in such a situation would imply the implementation of some form of "differentiated citizenship."[30]

Male and female attendance on Friday reflects the tradition of the country of attendees. While in some Muslim countries, it is customary for males only to attend these prayers, in others, both men and women attend. As a consequence of these cultural practices, gender representation in mosque attendance on Friday reflects the diversity of customary practices among Muslims in the United States.[31] In this light, adaptation to American society also implies adaptation to other Muslim practices and the diasporic regendering of the week according to different ethnic practices.

In addition, however, the changes experienced by diasporized Muslim women as part of the process of adaptation to the New York social landscape bring about a temporal difference between them and the women in the original country. Temporal change as a result of their participation in the Americanized Islamic week and the social mores of the American city dissociates them from temporal social practices in the homeland. So time is an issue that fractures the transnational relations between Americanized Muslim women and the homeland.[32]

The Muslim temporal enclave

The social processes at work among Muslim immigrants in New York City in part result in the periodic assimilation of these diasporas into the mainstream temporalities of the city. However, because the temporalities remain parallel, the opposite process also is at work. The subaltern temporalities are also transglobal. The presence of the transglobal in the local regime resists assimilation and leads over time to the transformation of the diasporans into an enclave city or chronopolis shaped by the modulations of Islamic temporal practices. This chronopolization takes various forms because of the interplay between the global and the local in the diasporans' specific localized niche.

The insertion of the five prayers within or into the interstices of the civil day gives Muslims "a very basic sense of Islamic identity"[33] separate from that imposed by the hegemonic civil day. Identity is not expressed in a temporal vacuum, and in the case of Muslims, not in any type of weekly arrangement. By giving a tempo to the day, the prayers constitute an infrastructure for the expression of that Islamic identity. The Islamic day, week, month, and year are all part of the architecture of this identity.

Islamic time is not civil time. The Islamic week and the civil week proceed from different assumptions, evolve according to different rhythms, and emphasize different aspects of the week. Naff[34] writes that "it had long been apparent to Muslims in the United States that the American time schedule and calendar were not adjusted to the Islamic way of life." The time of the "noon" prayer (*zuhr*), for example, varies from season to season or depending on the month of the year. The noon prayer was calculated to be held at 11:53 a.m. for November 1, 1998 and at 2:59 p.m. for September 29 of the same year for Muslims in the San Francisco Bay Area.

In the absence of the call to prayer by the muezzin, as happens in the Middle East, therefore, the Muslim immigrant in New York City becomes very attached to his or her watch and to the Islamic calendar, with its subdivision of daytime hours, to help locate when the prayers should be done. This calendar is needed not only to determine the time of midday prayers, because this does not always coincide with noon in the Western clock, but to identify the precise date and time of the beginning and ending of Ramadan and to verify the beginning of daylight in areas where fog can obstruct one's ability to see and determine the exact time of sunrise for morning prayers. The American Muslim calendar provides the time on the Western clock when the Muslim midday occurs and the precise time when each of the five prayers should be offered to Allah. The Western clock thus becomes an auxiliary for the identification of prayer times according to Muslim calculations. The temporal enclave of Muslim time takes precedence over civil time, and transglobal subaltern time displaces hegemonic time.

The disjunction between Islamic time and civil time is thus not simply a product of different histories, it is contemporary, as well.[35] Muslim temporalities and those of the hegemonic mainstream do not always mesh well, and the two cannot always be reconciled on the part of the subaltern community by strategies such as prayer clustering. While some employers are willing to let Muslims have time off for the Friday prayer because it is mandatory and because it happens once a week, for example, they are not always ready to allow time for the daily prayers. Unlike the congregational Friday prayers,

the daily prayers are acts of personal devotion and may not be noticeable to persons in the mainstream because of the shorter amount of
time they require. In contrast, the two to three hours prayer on Friday
require a longer and more visible absence from the workplace.

A Moroccan construction worker who is a regular at a recently constructed mosque in upper Manhattan – The Islamic Cultural Center
of New York – informed me that he takes his day off on Friday so
that he can come to the mosque for the congregational prayers. He
claims that he is not able to do his prayers at work because the boss
complains about the ten minutes he loses (or "wastes each time"),
since he is not allowed to work extra time because the office closes
at 5:00 p.m. It would be impractical for the manager to expand his
own hours to accommodate him. However, he indicated to me that
those who work for Arab American employers or even some Jewish
American employers are allowed to take time off for their prayers.

In some instances, though, strategies of temporal substitution are
possible and help assimilate Muslim to non-Muslim temporalities.
The manager of a textile store in Brooklyn who is of Palestinian
origin, but who does not own the store, informs me that he carefully
mixes Muslim with non-Muslim workers to prevent conflict on
Friday and during the month of Ramadan. On Friday, both the
manager and the Muslim workers leave the store at noon to attend
the midday prayers in a nearby mosque, and the non-Muslims run
the store while they are away. With this strategy, no profit is lost,
and the Muslim workers are able to fulfill their religious duties. In
some cases, arrangements are made on an ad hoc basis. That is, an
employee may request from an employer to start early on Friday so
that he can take time off at midday or may do overtime to compen-
sate for time lost at work. Similarly, a Turkish American faculty
member at a New York university had arranged with the college to
teach at 3:00 p.m. or in the morning so that he could attend the
Friday prayers at the nearby mosque in Manhattan. In the same vein,
students enrolled in universities try not to take classes that meet at
midday and early afternoon on Friday: "Very few," said a doctoral
student at one of the local universities, who is himself a devout
Palestinian Muslim, "unless that's a 'must-take' class so that you
might graduate, then they'll do it, but most will not take class on
Friday, usually after Friday prayer, that's when students gather, so
you'll most often see that will be the time of lunchtime gathering."

However, pursuing these strategies is not always possible. There are real problems associated with the practice of the Friday prayer. Haddad and Lummis[36] report that:

> Muslims . . . hesitate to ask their employers for time off to attend the Friday noon prayer service. This is due to the fear that such a request might hurt their chances of promotion or might be refused. One imam reported that his request for release from his job for two hours on Fridays to lead the Friday prayer was denied even though he was willing to have the necessary amount deducted from his salary.

A Saudi Arabian immigrant who has been living in the United States for the past 30 years confirms the incompatibility of Islamic and mainstream temporalities and the consequences that have flowed from them:

> If you want to pray on time you could probably get fired. Recently, they have been saying that there should be tolerance of Moslems if they want to pray, but until very recently, you could not pray during working hours unless you wanted to lose your job. And most of the time people do, from what I hear; it has never happened to me because I never prayed anyway. If you can't do it, Islam is flexible; you can pray later in the day or whenever you have the chance. So, even if you want to pray and feel good about your prayers, there is no place to go to. It is not allowed in the buildings; it is not allowed in the school. So, it is very lonely and intimidating if you are a practicing Moslem and you want to go pray at noon or at one o'clock. Your boss would not let you go; you would lose your job. And if the other two are available, there is no place where you could feel that you are at peace when you are praying.

Another Saudi confirmed this sense that the hegemonic culture is overtly hostile to the expression of Muslim temporalities:

> The Saudis who pray feel lonely when it comes to prayer time, extremely lonely, because they are in the environment that nobody prays except themselves. Maybe you will find one person

hiding behind a tree or behind a building praying on campus, and he also (mostly he, not she) knows that praying is being ridiculed in this culture . . . When you pray and you go to wash, when you go and do these rituals. So he is aware of two things: the fact that nobody next to him is praying, he does not even know if he is praying correctly or not. And he knows that the culture and the society are against Islam because of how Islam is being depicted in the American media, American TV, political campaigns, and stuff like that. So the ones who are actually faithful have a hell of a time praying in this country and normally some of them go back based on these kind of premises; because they cannot practice their faith freely like they do back home. I am not sure if it is freely, but safely. You know, in Saudi Arabia, everything stops at prayer time, and you go to pray whether you like it or not. Shops close, traffic stops . . . everything stops, and you go to the mosque. Here, you don't have that kind of collective prayers, efforts, and stuff like that.

Increasingly, however, there has been a recognition and acceptance of the fact that the temporalities of Islamic identity cannot be reduced to mainstream temporalities and that Islamic time forms a transglobalized enclave within mainstream time. As a result, American society has been bending its old ways to make room for Muslims[37] by providing space at the workplace for the congregational prayers and by converting work time into nonwork time so that the faithful can attend these prayers. Husain and Vogelaar have found that "most universities and colleges in Chicago provide rooms for Muslim students to offer Friday prayers. Many businesses and hospitals also provide space to conduct Friday prayers or allow time off to their Muslim employees to attend these prayer services."[38] For this to happen, there must be sufficient Muslim workers in the workplace or students attending the university for their request to be taken into consideration, either because of humanitarian concerns or because of a threat of discriminatory suits. Such a request may be granted irrespective of the existence of a nearby mosque and with the understanding that this disruption of work will not negatively affect the productivity of the operation.

Winning recognition as a legitimate temporal enclave has required negotiations in the workplace and in the broader fields of law, politics, and society. An imam who heads a mosque in the San Francisco Bay Area summed up the problem thus:

> I know that Oracle provides the room for Muslims who work in there as engineers, to pray in Silicon Valley. I know it has come up with many Muslims having to negotiate an hour or two to attend the prayer, and I think that's standard, and CAIR (Council on American Islamic Relations) has a whole advisory on worker's rights – which is this organization, and they have it on their website, their advice on how to approach and deal with this issue, and we have a list of the cases that they actually have won with companies that provided permission for their workers to attend the private prayer, and also issues of dress, beard, all those items. So they have many cases where the companies have agreed to that, it's a workers rights under religious need that the companies have to work with the workers to try to provide them that. Now there are definitely cases where the companies have difficulty accepting this and that's where the legal intervention has to be. But I know that Oracle does that and other companies in Silicon Valley, because there are large numbers of Muslim workers there.

In some places, the Muslims have been able to carve out micro-Islamic communities inside mainstream US society as a way of recouping the Islamic day and giving it a hegemonic status in their enclaved chronopolis. In Detroit's Southend, for example, just as in Arabic communities in the Middle East, calls for prayer "are now carried across a public address system, which can be heard throughout the area, reminding the Muslim residents of their obligations."[39] In Dearborn, Michigan, where the Muslim community is ghettoized, the call to prayer has become a permanent feature, which has occasioned objections by the surrounding community against the noise level in the area. Muslims in San Diego had also faced such a challenge. Hermansen[40] reports that "in the course of acquiring permission to build from the city a series of hearings were held" in which objectors "feared that the call to prayer would disturb the neighborhood." The presence of such a chronopolis not only establishes itself on the basis of its temporal difference, it thus affects the rest of the city as it pursues strategies to maintain its temporal distinctness.

In enclaves such as these, the subaltern day has emerged as an alternative to the hegemonic day, wholly recognized by the formal system to the extent that it has been able to impose its way in this specific niche.[41] Such enclaves, whether fully or only partially realized, function as genuine communities within communities – transglobalized chronopolises with links not shared with mainstream society. In my observations in two Manhattan mosques, I have found that the site of the Friday prayer is used as the place where the community meets as a group and where information about the community, discount stores, and political meetings affecting both the diaspora and the homeland are provided and shared. This phenomenon is not peculiar to New York. Those who have studied Muslim communities in other parts of the country have reported similar observations. For example, Fisher and Abedi[42] note that "prayer ends. Fliers are distributed: Five Star Groceries announces special prices; A&N Automobile and Body Shop, 10 percent off; Visit Shamania Sweets; Granny's Buffet invites everyone to a complete 'Id program with poetry and music . . .' There is no Iranian newspaper table. Rumor has it, they are at a demonstration today."

The difference between the weekly cycles of the enclave community and the mainstream society is manifest in the operation of stores located nearby mosques, where the owners anticipate clients will show up after Friday prayers. For these enclave businesses, Friday is a peak commercial day. One Muslim immigrant noted that:

> after the Friday prayer usually what happens is the businesses that are closely located around the mosque experience an increase in sales, an increase in commercial transactions; this is due to the proximity to the mosque, a lot of people attend the prayer, it affords them time to go to shop for the necessities, or what you call "ethnic food," or ethnic items that are not carried by the mainstream stores.

The transglobal chronopolis

As we have seen, because the Muslim diaspora follows a weekly cycle different from that of the civil week, both in its adaptations to that week as it runs parallel to it and in the resistances that constitute it as an enclave, it moves to its own rhythms engendered by Islamic temporal logic. This temporality structures the pace of life of the community and also affects various aspects of social and institutional life of the mainstream community. In addition, however, as we have also seen, the chronopolis it forms is not simply a local entity, but is also and foremost a transglobal production. Globality implodes in the local structure and in the process temporizes its behavioral expression.

The Muslim week has a global content in both its forward orientation and its backward posture. It is a continuation of the structure of the homeland week. Immigration simply implies a continuity of that practice, and in a sense transnationalizes and globalizes it. The Muslim living in New York is in temporal harmony with the homeland and with Muslims throughout the world as they are united by the temporal rhythms of their practice. The week is also global by the position of the faithful during the communal prayer facing Mecca, thereby recognizing the locational and spatial origin of their faith. One prays as if one were in Mecca, acknowledging the physical distance between here and there, but still in communion with the faithful everywhere and recognizing the geographical roots of one's faith.[43] Also, international connections with the homeland are sometimes maintained because some receive cassettes of sermons from abroad and listen to them on Friday at home or at the workplace, as some taxi drivers in New York do.

The distinct identity of the chronopolis is expressed at the local level when the entire community isolates itself from the mainstream for the purpose of fulfilling its religious obligations. At times during the course of the week, a good segment of New York city sets itself aside because Muslim workers are not available to carry out secular activities for themselves or mainstream employers. In this sense, their different temporal lifestyle fractures the social landscape, slowing down some activities in the formal economy and at the same time raising the intensity level of some sectors of the informal economy.

Three types of overt global intervention can be detected as they influence the form and content of the American-Muslim day. Perhaps the most visible sign of the implosion of the global in the local is manifest in the influence held by the homeland government over its overseas diasporas. The Saudi government goes as far as to provide the departee with a compass so that he or she may adequately locate geographically Mecca for the daily prayers:

Well, the Saudis give everybody this compass back home before they leave the country, and it shows you where Mecca is. So, wherever that compass needle refers to you go and pray; even if the compass is false, and the needle is directing them to the east, they would still pray wherever the needle shows them to pray.

Another way that the homeland government and clergy exert an overt presence in the transglobalized American Muslim chronopolis is by issuing the Islamic prayer calendar, which indicates the moments of the day and night when they are to be held, literally minute by minute. The calendar for the New York region was prepared by the Department of Survey and Geodesy of Cairo, Egypt and distributed in a booklet form to the faithful.[44]

The third form of overt intervention by the homeland is through the governance of the main mosque in Manhattan.[45] This influential mosque, which is a central point of gathering for Muslims living or working in New York City, is under the control of the Islamic states. The most visible sign of this control by the homelands is manifest through the role of its board of trustees, whose membership is made up of the permanent representatives of the Muslim countries at the United Nations. They have been influential in the selection and appointment of the imams, directors, and staff at this mosque. This type of managerial transnationality is consolidated by other types of diasporic transglobality (familial, grass-roots, congregational, professional, and industrial) among the rank and file of the chronopolis.

More covert interventions of the temporalities of the homeland in the Americanized Muslim chronopolis exist, as well. As one Iranian female student in the San Francisco Bay Area noted:

sometimes I'll see little flyers on the table when I'm walking out of the Friday prayer area, or when I'm at school, they have books and cassettes that you can borrow and bring back, but they're all related back to Islam and Muslim countries, there was an Internet printout – not something about sales or something that had nothing to do with the kind of building that you are in, it's really about politics, it's about Islamic politics, relating to Muslims.

Such unofficial irruptions of the homeland in the diasporized chronopolis can provide occasions for political opposition to and resistance directed at the forces governing the homeland. Because the Friday congregational prayer brings a large group of people to the mosque, it provides an opportunity for activists to promote opposition politics. In one of the San Diego mosques, "after one Friday prayer in 1993, for example, a leaflet was distributed by some disaffected persons (falsely) accusing this institution of being sponsored by the Saudi Arabian secret police."[46] The use of the congregational prayer both to spread state political propaganda or for opposition politics has always been a factor in the history of this institution.[47] Diasporization has not eclipsed such a practice. It has simply given diasporans one central means to reach the faithful and sensitize them to the political realities of the homeland, especially in communities that do not have their own radio programs and local newspapers.

Although opposition politics is one aspect of the politicization of the mosque, the faithful also use it to engage in what might be called "allegiance politics" and to support the government in office. Far from reducing the faithful to their religious dimension, the Friday service provides a site where the affairs of state are discussed among practitioners. It is the foremost site in the diaspora where Muslims with different ideological orientations address their political vision of the state.[48]

The informal economy also represents a covert presence of the homeland within the transglobalized diaspora. On Friday, from 10:00 a.m. to 3:00 p.m., the informal economy is alive and well in the areas in front of the main entrance of the Upper Manhattan Mosque. Vendors display their merchandise (Islamic books, carpets, jewelry, women clothing, incense, candles, videos, tape-recorded music, beads, and other homeland items) and attract a captive clientele to their ware. One finds here an ephemeral marketplace where homeland goods that are not available at this location in other days of the week can be purchased. Conversely, some mainstream secular or economic activities in the city are affected on Friday by the Muslim stores that are not available and professional offices that are not open for business. Thus, as in the Jewish American chronopolis, but in distinctively different ways, the adaptations and resistances of transglobalized diasporic Muslim temporalities within the structure of the subaltern week constitute a separate temporal enclave within the civil society of New York City. As we will now see, in each case, the ramifications of these temporal differences extend to the ways in which citizens of these chronopolises inhabit the larger temporal cycles, as well.

5
Subaltern and Hegemonic Holidays

The temporal disjuncture of some ethnic weekly cycles in relation to the civil week that we have examined thus far is just one aspect of a larger problem of multicultural asynchronization. The yearly cycle is another aspect of this temporal disjuncture. New York city is traversed by several diasporic new years and other annual holidays that do not coincide with the official American New Year's Day of the Gregorian calendar, with the official holidays of the state and federal government, or with each other. The Chinese celebrate the advent of their new year in February, the Iranians in March, and the Jews in September, for example.

Even the date of the year itself is asynchronous. For Christians, the date of the year is in reference to the birth of Jesus. For Jews, the date of the year is in relation to the creation of the world by God, believed to be on what, in the Christian calendar, would be Monday, October 7, 3761 BC.[1] For Muslims, the date corresponds with the flight of the Prophet Mohammed from Mecca to Medina in what would be 622 AD.

One must also distinguish between two types of ethnic new years: the routine new year that is punctuated in the calendar once a year, and the millennial new year that makes its appearance every thousand years. There is asynchronicity between the routine mainstream new year and some ethnic new years because they do not begin on the same day. However, this temporal disharmony is more apparent when a chronopolis is celebrating a millennial year and the mainstream is not, or vice versa. The new millennial year for the West is not a millennium for much of the Rest. For the Muslims, the year

2000 corresponds to the year 1420 of Hegira; for the Jews, it is year 5760; and for the Chinese it is the Year of the Dragon 4696. The millennial new year is one example where the temporal disparity between a chronopolis and the mainstream is magnified tenfold. Furthermore, one must make a distinction between ethnic holidays that are religious holy days, such as Eid al-Fitr and Eid al-Adha celebrated at the end of Ramadan and at the end of the pilgrimage to Mecca, and secular holidays such as national independence days.

Ethnic new years, holy days, and holidays are celebrated as special days by diasporans, and in some cases they last more than a day or a week. Some of these festivals are so spectacular (the Chinese New Year, for instance) that the city cannot help but be aware of their occurrence. Yet, other holidays are known almost exclusively to the specific ethnic group that celebrates the event – Dominican Independence day, for example. There are many factors that contribute to this exclusivity, such as recent immigration to New York, the small size of the ethnic community, or the marginalization of such celebrations, even in the homeland, as in the case of the Indo-Trinidadian divali festival.[2] Not all ethnic holidays are of equal significance to the diasporans, of course. Just as mainstream holidays are stratified in terms of their religious and secular importance – the Martin Luther King holiday, for example, does not match in spirit and festivity the Christmas, Fourth of July, or Thanksgiving holidays in the United States – so are ethnic holidays. For example, among Jewish Americans, Purim, Shavuot, and Simchat Torah are not celebrated in a solemn way similar to the observances of Yom Kippur, Rosh Hashanah, or the first day of Pesach. This stratification is related to the event each represents and to their importance in the lives of the people.

Whether or not the mainstream is aware of these diasporic new years and subaltern holidays, taken together, they are markers of identity for ethnic communities and regulate the temporality of their diasporic life. As Jacobs recalls, "I grew up, nominally Jewish on Sundays and on the Jewish holidays, like Rosh Hashanah and Yom Kippur, when we stayed away from public schools."[3] Dolph Schayes, member of the Basketball Hall of Fame and once coach of Buffalo Braves, has similar reminiscences about growing up as a Jewish youngster in the Bronx: "we stayed away from school on the high holidays."[4] Subaltern diasporic holidays provide a temporal niche for the incubation, expression, and reproduction of ethnic identity and an immigrant group's cultural heritage. But they are also an arena where conflict over the performance of one's identity resonates because of the different and sometimes contradictory expectations from co-ethnics, school, the community at large, and one's religion.

The study of ethnic holidays has been approached from different angles, which has led to productive perspectives that shed light on the temporality of their incorporation in the American city.[5] In fact, these holidays are privileged moments that identify the cultural temporality of the group, that express both difference and integration, that reflect ethnic resistance, and that symbolically prioritize the subalternized temporality of the immigrant community over the hegemonic temporality of the dominant sector of society.

So far, the sociology of ethnic holidays has focused primarily on location (the appropriation of mainstream space), difference (the relations of the group with the mainstream system), integration (behavioral and ideological assimilation), meaning and representation (the reproblematization of the cultural event in a foreign land, outside its original niche) and celebration (the ludic, mythic, and symbolic aspects of holidays). The myriad ethnic holidays have been regarded as a public performance of ethnic identity and a reinterpretation of historical memories;[6] as encoding the memory of the group;[7] as a medium for the socialization of youngsters in the group's cultural heritage;[8] as resistance to complete assimilation;[9] as an inversion of power through the imposition of ethnic holidays over the temporality of the mainstream;[10] as a cultural expression of "informal nationalism" essential for the sustenance of formal nationalism;[11] and as a form of identification with the homeland.[12] Other studies have focused on how and why minor holidays in the homeland become more elaborate rituals in the diaspora as a way of performing ethnic pride;[13] how diasporic citizens appropriate national symbols of their country of adoption and incorporate them in the expression of their holiday celebrations;[14] how ethnic associations play an important role in the organization of ethnic holiday celebrations;[15] and how the meaning of ethnic holiday celebrations changes from one period to another because of the evolving relations between the country of adoption and the homeland.[16] It is obvious that these ethnic events are not pure artifacts, but are concocted out of the local environment using traditions with cultural roots in the homeland.

This chapter, like the preceding ones, will focus on the interactions between the holidays of the subalternized temporality and the holidays enforced by the hegemonic mainstream temporalities – on how diasporans inscribe their holidays in the architecture of their own and mainstream communities. These ethnic holidays are interpreted as temporal events that anchor the diasporic chronopolises in both the mainstream and the homeland. Diasporic new years and holidays are interpreted here as genuine temporal sites where the global is apprehended, domesticated, and localized. As collective events, they are engines of social change. The diasporic new years and holidays carry bundles of global meanings that are reflected in structural change in the celebratory event itself – because of change, for example, in the history of the homeland – and in the relations of the diaspora with the receiving country, in changes of the attitude of the mainstream *vis-à-vis* the ethnics. In large part, this is due to the change in the history of the receiving country (civil rights movements, the celebration of diversity), and to technological change that makes transnationality a reality. As important temporal sites, these holidays not only cadence the rhythms of each chronopolis, but also shape the identity of each in terms of distinguishing it both from the mainstream and from other ethnic communities or chronopolises.

Diasporic temporal practices

The diasporic new year as the local expression of a global reality is the temporal anchor that provides a cadence to diasporic life. It identifies the hegemony of the diasporic yearly cycle inside the chronopolis, it serves as a compass to locate the other subaltern holidays celebrated by the ethnic community, and, in some calendars, it even serves to explain the identity of the year. For example, the Chinese identify their years with animal names that evoke the fundamental content of the year and what individuals born in that year should expect later in life. But the new year as a point of departure also accentuates the closing of a period or a seasonal cycle and the celebration of the beginning of a new cycle. Such an important event not only has symbolic significance, but also practical implications, especially in the commercial arena.

The ethnic new year is, after all, both an ethnic and familial celebration. Such a special ethnic day is inserted inside a social structure different from that of the sending society and is both an adaptation and a new temporal creation. This is a specific moment when the traditions of the homeland are revived, retrieved, relived, and transmitted from one generation to the next. The performance of traditions that express different temporalities and showcase different cultural practices separates ethnics from the mainstream. It is a communal time because it is not simply family traditions that are retrieved, but also country or national traditions. Subaltern time opens a niche inside the formal temporality of the mainstream and appropriates that niche for itself, bringing asynchronicity to the whole urban system. These different times bring different flows of activity to mark the specificity of these moments.

For example, the Muslim American yearly cycle is punctuated according to the Islamic calendar by two major holy days, "the id al-fitr, the feast of the breaking of the fast which falls at the end of the month of Ramadan, the tenth month of the Muslim calendar, and the id al-adha, the feast of the sacrifice, which occurs at the climax of the hajj (pilgrimage) in the twelfth month of the Muslim calendar."[17] These holy days remain ethnic events because they are not celebrated by the majority of the population and more often than not are not even noticed by non-Muslims. For this reason, "Muslim students are not excused from classes, nor are workers given a day off to participate in these celebrations."[18] Haddad[19] reports that in regard to these holidays, Dearborn, Michigan is an exception to the rest of the United States because there "the holidays are recognized semi-officially." This is made possible because of the large concentration of Muslims in that city.

The practice of diasporic holidays varies from one group to another, within a given group, and from one generation to the next. The intensity of such a practice may also vary, whether it is a secular or religious holiday. We can get a sense of these generational variations from a middle-aged Jewish woman who reminisces about her participation in the Jewish holidays as a young girl growing up in New York and later as a married woman in the San Francisco Bay Area:

Okay, the holiday starts at sundown on the night before, and on both of those holidays [Rosh Hannah and Yom Kippur], we would have a big meal. On Rosh Hashanah, we would have a big meal, and the next day we would spend almost all day in the synagogue. This was very boring for kids because it was all in Hebrew. We belonged to a conservative synagogue. These two holidays were the only days we went to synagogue. We didn't go on Saturdays, and as a child, I just had to sit there and not know a word of what they were saying. Nothing was in English, and then I think we went home for lunch and then came back again. A lot of people gathered outside of the synagogue and didn't go in. It was kind of social, like we got to hang out with our friends, and then we had another meal that night. It was all planned and prepared days ahead, because on Rosh Hashanah *you really* didn't do anything. We couldn't do anything. We dressed up and sat on the bench outside and that's about it. During Rosh Hashanah we did this for two days. Yom Kippur was even more intense. We had a big meal the night before, before sundown, because sundown is when the holiday officially starts. On Yom Kippur, from sundown that night until sundown the next day, you couldn't eat anything. So you kind of had to stock up. So we also went to synagogue on Yom Kippur, we were there all day, and we didn't eat anything, except actually, I think, when you're 13 you started fasting, but if you were younger than that you could eat. But it was kind of fun for us to see if we could fast all day without eating anything. Also, we didn't meet with other families or anything, we just fasted with our own families. When we broke the fast, we had a light meal, since we hadn't put anything in our stomachs all day. We ate things like herring, egg salad, just a light meal. Now we only do one day of Rosh Hashanah. My parents still do two. But, I think reform Jews only do one. And I don't know what we are.

A Muslim Iranian woman likewise describes the activities she regularly carries out during the celebrations of the diasporic new year as both a family and community affair:

The New Year celebrations last 13 days and begin on March 20. Every day we have special sweets, and during this period, we convey our best wishes to family members and friends, and on the thirteenth day we go and celebrate. For instance, we have a picnic in a park and throw out some vegetables and say "Bad luck and go away." So basically the first day is a family celebration, and the last day is more a group event. If the last day falls during the week, we prefer to postpone the celebrations for the following weekend. On the first day of the Iranian new year, I usually called my parents in Teheran to wish them a happy new year. I like to celebrate our new year. I routinely do it with my aunt. She always invites me, she knows I like it, so I give her a gift on the new year, she gives me a gift. We are the only members of the family in New York.

Her practice of the event corroborates the occurrence of the transfer of the dates from a work day to the weekend, the intensity of transnational relations, the multinationalization of the immigrant family, and the transnationalization of the celebration itself with the long-distance participation of family members at home and abroad.

The ethnic new year contrasts with the American New Year's Day, but the mainstream community is not always aware of the existence of such celebrations among diasporans. Although the new year celebrations are different and located in a different position or separate time frame *vis-à-vis* the mainstream new year, they are a *habitus* for the ethnics.[20] Self-fulfilled consciousness characterizes the ethnic new year because it is a time of celebratory otherness or the celebration of the communal self. It is a time of ethnic consciousness that makes one aware of one's difference because it is internally propelled, and not externally imposed.

The holidays allow an opportunity for the group to reconstitute itself as a separate entity inside the mainstream. Memories of the place of birth are revived, new friendships are developed, news about the homeland is shared, diasporic culture is transmitted to the younger generation, programs to help the poor at home and abroad are concocted, and diasporic solidarity in its multiple forms is expressed.

One should not propagate the erroneous idea that these celebratory ethnic events always bring harmony in the group. They are sometimes objects of dissension in themselves or provide a context for airing dissent. Meijers[21] notes that "there have . . . always been orthodox groups which have refused to celebrate independence day. Their argument is that the Jews should not have established the state before the coming of the Messiah." There are, then, contested holidays. While the holidays tend to allow the group to renew itself and reinvigorate its traditions, it can also be a period of intense ideological conflict because a segment may contest the validity of such a celebration. In other words, some may refuse to take part in such holidays for ideological reasons.

Diasporic holidays may reflect homeland temporal conflicts. These conflicts are not the production of the diasporic condition, but reflect the cultural continuity and attachment of the diaspora to the homeland. I have in mind the asynchronicity of the temporalities of both the Eastern Orthodox Church and the Roman Catholic Church in New York in regard to the celebration of Christmas and Easter. Since the Eastern church did not accept the Gregorian reform, Easter is celebrated at different times by immigrant Christians who belong to either of these two churches. This asynchronicity has its origins in the homeland, but is choreographed in the immigrant country.

Because diasporic temporalities are the result of subsidiarization, conflict in the homeland continues to affect the diaspora. This is so because, in the example just cited, the headquarters of the church is in charge of establishing policies for satellite or subsidiary churches. The Orthodox Church in New York celebrates Christmas on January 7 because they are the offshoot of a central church located elsewhere. The diasporic community affiliated with the church cannot solve this temporal problem locally because it is part of a global temporal regime and rhythm.

Furthermore, the celebration of ethnic holidays is not always on a par with the homeland cultural time because sometimes they are commemorated on different days. This is so because the homeland holidays may not be holidays in New York, and therefore these local celebrations need to be postponed to a different date, which may desynchronize them with the homeland temporal rhythm. Sometimes temporal relocation of the diasporic holidays causes a partial and not total desynchronization with the homeland or the transnational temporal flow, because during the evening, the immigrants may still listen to a speech from the president or prime minister (or to the homily of the national religious leader) if it is broadcast on ethnic TV or radio, and through these media partake in the mainland celebrations. The same phenomenon of asynchronization may occur when the celebrations are postponed to another day in the homeland and not in the diaspora.

Achelis[22] makes a major analytical distinction when she distinguishes "date holidays" from "day holidays." Date holidays may happen any day of the week, since the dates for days change every year. If October 10 is a Monday this year, it will be a Tuesday next year. The day may vary, but not the date as in the case of the Fourth of July. In contrast, day holidays are fixed days, no matter what their date is. For example, each year, the Labor Day holiday is celebrated on the first Monday in September. The date varies, but the day does not. To these distinctions, one must add "substitute day holidays," which refers to the relocation of a holiday to another day to accommodate the work schedule of participants. Substitute day holidays occur when such holidays are occasionally transferred to other days, such as the weekend. Because of work, these holidays are not celebrated on the exact days, especially if such a celebration involves or is dependent on public participation.

Participation in mainstream and ethnic holidays

Ethnic holidays are local sites in which two global temporal flows intersect as they globalize the relationship of one to the other, and, in the process, transglobalize the structure, content, and meaning of such festive practices. One must then see the ethnic holiday as a hybrid temporal phenomenon whose global meaning is constructed out of the global infrastructure of its local practices. The ethnic holiday is one privileged site where globality shows its local face.

The local interaction of these globalized temporal flows is mediated by power. These are not relationships undertaken by two groups of equal strength, but rather by a dominant and subaltern group. Social class, gender, or race is invoked at the point of the inscription of the global in the local for the management of the interaction between two cultural groups. We must therefore pay attention to the nature and working of subalternity in the everyday practices of nonhegemonic diasporic communities.

The ethnic holiday is subalternized because it is not recognized by the state as a state holiday and therefore remains in the domain of the ethnic group. It is subalternized not because it is an ethnic phenomenon, but because the group lacks power to impose its festivities on the mainstream. So it is not a question of ethnicity, but of the power and the demographic strength of the group. I mention the demographic factor because on diasporic holidays, neighborhood strength can affect such things as class attendance, paralyzing the local school system. Diasporic holidays can be subalternized whether the diaspora emanates from the West or the Rest. Although French immigrants belong to the dominant Euro American community because of their European ancestry, their holidays are nevertheless minoritized and subalternized. They are majoritized in terms of race and minoritized in terms of temporalities. Bastille Day in San Francisco is not a holiday, even though the French celebrate in the streets of the city with non-French revelers. Although not recognized as an official state holiday, such a holiday may still attract the attention of outsiders if the ethnics put on a show, as in the case of the parade organized by Mexican American groups to celebrate the Cinco de Mayo festivities, for example.

Under what circumstances can we expect events in the diaspora, in their position of subalternity, to emerge as part of the mainstream activities? Do the subaltern push their way into and colonize the mainstream with their festive activities? Are the subaltern events co-opted by the mainstream? What kinds of genealogy is developed in the margins?

Ethnic holidays are holidays in the minds of the diasporic population, but they are also a materially celebrated practice. In areas where the ethnic population is dense, they may be able to convert their ethnic holidays into city holidays.

Since they are living in the United States, diasporic communities must confront the mainstream holidays. Their responses to such events are part of their integration in American society. Thus, for example, "One of the realities of being Muslim in the American context is having to decide whether or not to celebrate holidays that are part of the American and often specifically the Christian calendar." With regard to the sometimes raucous American New Year's Eve celebrations, "Most Muslims interviewed . . . saw no reason not to observe the Western new year as long as it does not mean joining the celebrations 'with a lot of alcohol and a lot of dancing and a lot of other non-Islamic behavior which goes on.' Seeing the new year in with friends and family and perhaps having a family gathering on New Year's Day are activities many Muslims engage in."[23]

In his study of Iranian immigrants in Iowa, Chaichian notes that about half the Iranians in his Iowa City sample celebrate or observe American religious and secular holidays, such as Christmas, Halloween, or Thanksgiving. Many, especially women, adore Christmas trees and their ornamental and decorative beauty, and one can find Christmas trees in some Muslim homes during the holiday season. Several respondents indicated that they observe American holidays only "for the sake of their children," so that they are not left alone and isolated from American children who normally observe these events.[24]

Ethnic participation in mainstream holidays varies greatly depending on the level of assimilation of the group, which may be affected by generational factors and may reveal a good deal of indeterminacy and ambivalence. A middle-aged Jewish New Yorker recalls how she and her parents have related to these mainstream holidays, both Christian and secular:

When I was a kid, I mean, Christmas wasn't any special day for us, at all. We'd just look out and say "look at all those kids playing with their new bicycles." Well, my best friend was not Jewish, my best friend Colette, so I got to help her decorate her Christmas tree, and then we exchanged gifts. But we didn't do anything special on Christmas day. But since my parents didn't go to work, since everything was closed, it was more like a Sunday, I guess, where you just kind of hang out, maybe visit relatives. But I don't really have any memories of Christmas.

There was no way I would even have considered asking for a Christmas tree. I mean, it just wouldn't enter my mind – it was not to be mentioned. But, we did have Christmas stockings at least one year that I remember. I think they were those mesh bags with candy already in them – I don't know. Yet, I do have a memory of Christmas stockings, and I don't know why she let us have those because we didn't celebrate Christmas, and to them anything Christian was really a big no-no. Even though – or you could say Christmas is kind of celebrated in America as just an American nonsectarian holiday. But they didn't see it that way. Yeah, no, we never had a Christmas tree.

We still don't have a Christmas tree because I'm married to someone Jewish who would really be offended by having a Christmas tree. Even though a Christmas tree is really a symbol of the winter solstice. But I do remember, when my daughter was young, we had Christmas trees. Certain Jewish friends of ours wouldn't come over because they didn't want their kids to see it and want a Christmas tree and have to deal with their kids. When I tell people, when I tell my Jewish friends, that I really like Christmas, it's like blasphemy – like you're not supposed to like Christmas if you're Jewish. You know, it's like, the birth of Christ. Actually, for Christmas now, we hang up stockings in our house, and on Christmas Eve we make hot chocolate and we get in our car and we drive around and we look at all the Christmas lights that people put up on their houses. And my son, who's ten years old, believes in Santa Claus. And we hang things in our Christmas stockings for him to recoup the next day.

We celebrated Valentines Day, we celebrated Halloween. My parents didn't see those as Christian holidays at all. But, Easter I remember we dyed Easter eggs, for some reason my mother let us do that. We always dyed Easter eggs. My mother always made a point of pointing out people in their Easter bonnets and their Easter clothes, because in New York, for some reason, people got really dressed up on Easter. That was like the thing to do. The Easter parade – we watched the Easter parade on TV. And on Fifth Avenue there was always an Easter parade and that was like the thing, for people to have their new spring clothes on, new shoes, new dresses.

Ethnic groups and families vary in the ways they relate to the mainstream and diasporic holidays. For example, Jacobs recalls that "even in our home Christmas was a more important holiday than Chanukah."[25] In contrast, Pogrebin remarks that "the Jewish New Year was the real new year; January First some pagan imitation."[26] Most Jews, however, participate in both new years, if not for themselves, for the sake or under pressure from their children. Depending on their attachment to their religious precepts or level of assimilation to the mainstream culture, they may participate more in their ethnic holidays than in the American holidays, or more in the American holidays than in their ethnic holidays, or equally in both.

Ethnic holidays as markers of identity

Diasporic identity is transnational partly because it is molded by transnational global flows, which have their own varied architecture at the local level. In this sense, ethnic holidays are a manifestation of the global anchorage of local diasporic temporal identitary practices.

In particular, the association between particular ethnic holidays and particular ethnic food practices constructs ethnic identity out of the temporality of the ethnic calendars: special types of food for specific types of calendrical events. The ethnic calendar both reflects and regulates food behavior. Ethnic food intake has temporal meanings that are articulated with the temporality of the diasporas. The food prepared and served for the special occasion is different from that used during the ordinary days of the year. Sorin points out that "almost every religious holiday celebrated by Jews involved a special food or beverage: matzo (unleavened bread) and gefilte fish on Passover, hamantash (three-cornered pastry filled with fruit or poppy seeds) at Purim, and challah (egg bread) for the traditional Sabbath meal on Friday evenings."[27] But the preparation and consumption of special foods quickly ramify into a host of other practices and behaviors that construct a particular ethnic identity:

Okay, well, like Yom Kippur, like I said we were served a light meal. But, for Rosh Hashanah I think my mom made chicken or roast beef or something like that. This was the main part of the meal and, I don't think there are really specific foods for Rosh Hashanah. It's just – Oh yeah, I just remember, you're supposed to eat apples and honey. To symbolize a sweet year, you dip apples in honey. Also, for every Jewish holiday, except for Passover, starting on the Sabbath on Friday night, you have Challah, you know, egg bread, braided egg bread. It's traditional. What do you call it? Celebratory bread or something. That's just, must be just tradition because I don't think it's written down anywhere that you have to have that bread. But Rosh Hashanah eve, Yom Kippur eve, and the Sabbath, and Passover, that's the holiday tradition.

So Passover was the big food holiday, because we couldn't eat bread or anything made with wheat flower or most other grains. We couldn't eat rice or oats. We had to buy special food. Every grocery store had a special section with Passover food, and the main food was matzo that we used as a bread substitute. It was like a cracker. It was unleavened bread, you know, having to do with the story of Passover, how the Jews had to leave Egypt and didn't have time to let their bread rise, and so they had these flat board breads, matzo. One of the other things on Passover was the meal, made from ground-up matzos, called matzo meal. You could make matzo balls with it. That was basically it. It's different now because they have all these things that are kosher for Passover prepackaged. Things like brownies, and cookies, that they make with matzo flour, I guess. But in the fifties, they really didn't have all that stuff. So it was pretty boring for a week. Plus, you did have to go to school, except for, I think the first two days of Passover you didn't go to school. But, when you went to school, what was in your lunch? Matzos with cream cheese. And they were kind of soggy by the time you ate them. So, you had a lot of matzos. It was hard going to school and having to have that. You couldn't have sandwiches.

But I was going to say something else about Passover – not only could you not eat bread and all those forbidden foods, you had to change all of your dishes. We had a totally different set of dishes, and not just one different set of dishes – we had separate dishes for meat dishes and nonmeat dishes. The meat dishes are called *fleishich*, and the nonmeat are called *milchik, milidich*, or something. During the year, you had these two separate sets of dishes, and then on Passover you had two other separate sets of dishes. And different dish drainers, different table clothes. Also we were supposed to get all the bread products – all the leavened products, and all the forbidden food out of our house, throw it away. We couldn't keep it in the house. So when everything was out my mom had dish towels over the counters with all the food out in special plates and a few glasses because she couldn't have two complete sets of dishes, but I don't even know where she kept it. We lived in apartments, she must have stored it away someplace. Different silverware and everything.

The other thing that I have found out is that there are the Ashkenazi Jews, who are the ones who came from Eastern Europe. That's where we're from. There's the Sephardic Jews who come from, like, Africa and Spain, and just other places in the world, who eat rice, who eat other grains, like oats. I'm not sure what they eat, but I know they eat rice on Passover, and so now I've started feeling like it's okay to eat rice on Passover, because it's not a law, it's not any Jewish law, its just the way the different types of Jews do it. Like the Ashkenazi Jews – you don't have legumes. That means you can't have peanuts, peanut butter, soybeans, any soybean product, but you know, we're not that religious anyway, so we eat all those things. And some people just don't eat bread, like Miriam's family, they don't eat bread, but they eat everything else: cookies, cake, anything. It's more symbolic for them, I guess.

Back in New York it was really easy to get all that stuff. Here, it's not as easy. I've driven down to Molly Stone's in Marin because they have lots of stuff. Like macaroons, one of the special treats are macaroons, little coconut cookies, and, actually matzo balls are a big treat, I think. I can't remember the other things – oh, chocolate-covered matzos, matzos any way you could think of it.

They have separate bags because some people really don't want their Passover things touching anything else. Yeah. Some people I know in Santa Rosa, in an effort to get their local stores to carry more Passover food, try to, you know, shop at the local stores and, you know, patronize them, so that the stores feel like it's worth their while to carry that stuff. And sometimes I think that I should do that, too. Certain stores, in certain neighborhoods, even in Santa Rosa, are better than others, where there's a larger Jewish population.

Chanukah food. Okay. Chanukah food, the main thing about Chanukah is one of the holidays where you don't light the Shabbas candles. You don't, you know, you don't light the candles and have the Challah thing. It's the Chanukah candles, it's a whole different candle thing. The menorah has nine candles in it, the one candle is the special candle that you use to light all the others with. And so the first night of Chanukah, you light one candle, the second night two, the third night three, etcetera. So Chanukah goes for eight nights and the main thing is to eat things cooked in oil because it's the miracle of the oil lasting for eight days when they only thought it would last for one. And so, in America, it's potato pancakes, we call potato latkes, that are fried in oil. In Israel, it's jelly donuts. Yeah, that's their Passover. Well no, that would be like, say, you'd have that for desert. No, they wouldn't eat that for dinner, but, say, you'd make sure you had jelly donuts, and if you maybe went to a Chanukah party, you'd have a lot of jelly donuts. Where in America you'd have a lot of potato latkes. But the main thing is the oil. That's really it. So everybody has their own way of doing it.

You can't really buy them ready-made. They have to be hot, piping hot. They're not good if they've gotten cold even. Some people make them ahead, 'cause usually if you're going to have a Chanukah party, or you're going to invite people, you'd be standing there cooking them for hours, so some people do make them ahead, and freeze them or refrigerate them and then heat them up again. And in synagogues they have big Chanukah parties where they make like millions of potato latkes, and they get all these women to come and help them cook potato latkes days ahead.

This statement illustrates not just how the Jewish yearly cycle is punctuated by a series of holidays from Rosh Hashanah through Yom Kippur, and Hanukkah to Passover, but how the identity of the participants in each of these events is expressed through culinary practices that connect with the geography or spatial arena for the display of such identities: the household, the synagogue, stores where kosher food items can be purchased. Other informants might add to these the front of the synagogue for those who do not want to get in, the park where one meditates and kills time on a fast day, and the *eruv* that provides an extension of the private domain. This geography has different boundaries from the one used in the routine periods, which put more emphasis on the household, school sites, workplace, and commuting. One thus may distinguish the high moments of ethnic identification during ethnic holidays from the routine periods and the relations of one to the other in the temporal expression of that identity.

Another aspect that distinguishes the construction of identity during these special days is increased attendance at ceremonies of worship. Thus, "Participation in synagogue services was especially noticeable during the Jewish High Holy Days of Rosh Hashanah and Yom Kippur. Indeed in many cities during the Holy Days, congregations could not accommodate all who wished to attend services. On the Lower East Side of New York in 1917, for example, it was necessary prior to Rosh Hashanah to create hundreds of temporary synagogues."[28]

The identities constructed in and through the observance of these ethnic holidays sometimes have been inflected by the proximity of ethnic holidays to mainstream observances and by their subaltern position in American society. Their theological significance does not change, but they become more elaborate performances. "The fact that Hanukkah, a minor religious holiday, has assumed such importance is due to its proximity to Christmas and reflects the ethnic communal need to have something Jewish to offer children in the holiday season."[29] Not just any ethnic holiday may develop such a propensity, but only those that have some affinity to mainstream holidays. Hanukkah, a festival of lights, blends nicely with the pageantry of Christmas in Western Christianity. A married Jewish woman remarks that:

> Sometimes Chanukah and Christmas overlap; usually Chanukah is ahead of Christmas, we give a gift, usually give a gift each night. Different people do it differently. Some people give all their gifts one night. Some people save the big gift for last, some people just give a bunch of small gifts. When I was a kid, we got very small gifts; Chanukah was not a major gift-giving holiday like Christmas was, it's just gotten more that way.

Proximity to a mainstream holiday may also trivialize the ethnic holiday and subvert the construction of ethnic difference. The rise in status of an ethnic holiday occurs when the ethnics concentrate their attention on their holiday and upholds it in competition with the mainstream. In contrast, when the ethnics take part in both, and when the ethnic holiday follows the mainstream holiday, such an ethnic holiday may lose its importance among the adult members of the group, with a corresponding loss in a sense of distinctive otherness. The *New York Times* of December 1, 1994 reports that "the Jewish calendar has rendered Hanukkah missing in action: already more than halfway gone, it's an afterthought to Thanksgiving rather than an alternative to the big Yuletide show. Jews who are still coping with turkey and brisket leftovers may not be up for dreidel-spinning. Nor, perhaps, are they eager for another elaborate family gathering at which certain in-laws might reopen hostilities brought to an easy cease-fire only last Thursday."

Some ethnic holidays acquire new meanings over the years. It is not simply a question of change of significance, as happens in the Filipinos' Rizal Day, but an accumulation of meanings because another celebration is added to the first one. When the Israelis decided to celebrate their independence day on Yom Kippur, they invested that day with a new meaning, one associated with the identity of the nation-state, as well as with the identity of a people. "The Holy Days of Judaism and the secular holidays of the Jewish people merge into one another. A religious quality is associated with the newest of Jewish holidays, Israel Independence Day (Yom ha-atzmaut), even as a national and ethnic motif is present in the holiest of Jewish Holy Days, the Day of Atonement (Yom Kippur)."[30] But since such a merger was not a result of a consensus, but a state's decision, some members of the Jewish diaspora celebrate Yom Kippur, but not necessarily independence day.

Business and diasporic holidays

The ethnic new year is a period of intense activities during which the chronopolis attracts tourists, non-ethnics, and nonghettoized co-ethnics. It is a period during which transnational economic transactions are more intense among ethnic businessmen as items are purchased abroad to be resold in the enclave. Co-ethnics come to buy these items, which are not necessarily produced in the enclave, but are rather imported from the homeland. Ethnic enclaves thus use ethnic holidays to make a profit. The economic side of these holidays cannot be overestimated because the ethnic business cycles are related to the holidays. This is a time when ethnic items are sold in large quantities, when the agglomeration economy gets a boost, and when small retailers crowd the streets to make a profit as well.

Depending on the size of the group, these holidays may also have a negative effect on the economic life of the neighborhood because ethnic stores may remain closed on holy days and ethnic employees may not be available for work or may simply rework their working hours. In one study of Moslems, "Most of those interviewed . . . said that there is no problem taking the Eids as holidays as long as the time is made up or counted as experience."[31] The following

Jewish example provides an insider's view of the problem of observing the Jewish holidays within the temporalities of the hegemonic calendar:

> My father was a dry cleaner, so you know, you just knew, you took those days off, and it was understood. When he had his own business, his own dry cleaning business, he closed, he just closed those days. My mom took off work. The company she worked for was a construction company, Tishman Realty and Construction Company, and they were Jewish, so they probably closed. They probably closed.
>
> Now my husband, Tom, does not go to work on Rosh Hashanah and Yom Kippur. I made him take off. Well, I said to Tom, because we have a ten year-old son, who we're raising Jewish and I think we need to be the example, so if you want your son to think it's an important holiday, then you have to take off. So I think the first couple of years we were married he didn't take off, and then he started, and now he takes off.
>
> Oh yeah, well if, when I worked at Hewlett Packard, to take time off on Rosh Hashanah or Yom Kippur, I just used my vacation time. Um yeah, where back East I think it's different, it's just like half the office is gone. But here, it's just, you just take your own personal time, to take off, if you want to do that, you know, just like any other day you'd want to take off for vacation. That's how it would be.

Even in places like New York, however, these ethnic holidays minimally affect the mainstream community, since the major commercial institutions do business as usual on those days. But these festivities do not pass unnoticed by the mainstream community: "And most people continued doing what they were doing on a mild morning in a city slowed somewhat by the Jewish New Year. Rosh Hashanah," the *New York Times* noted.[32]

Ethnic holidays and school closing

Ethnic holidays may be noted by representatives of the mainstream temporality, but accommodation of such holidays by mainstream institutions depends on the presence of enough diasporans to exert influence on the dominant centers of power. Whether or not schools close for ethnic holidays provides a convenient illustration of the ways in which such institutional recognition is achieved.

What strikes an observer of the public school system in New York is the number of holidays during which schools are closed. In addition to major legal holidays, such as Labor Day and Thanksgiving, the schools are closed on major Christian and Jewish holidays, but not yet on Muslim holidays. Until 1960, only Christian holidays such as Christmas and Good Friday were incorporated as school holidays in the New York City school districts. Even in neighborhood schools with a sizable number of Jewish students, these Christian holidays were imposed on them while the Board of Education completely ignored Jewish holidays. Of course, this was the era when assimilation to Anglo-Saxon culture and the Christian faith was seen as intrinsic to being an ideal American.

> In 1928, the Board granted a request by Herbert Goldstein, president of the Union of Orthodox Jewish Congregations, to change the Easter vacation schedule to begin on the first day of Passover rather than on Good Friday. However, Jewish attempts to gain recognition for Rosh Hashanah and Yom Kippur failed. When the Federation of Jewish Women's Organizations asked for the end of Friday night graduations in 1922, the Board of Education left the decision to the local district superintendents and public school principals . . . These remained neighborhood initiatives and did not spread throughout the city's Jewish section.[33]

The Jewish population was doubly affected because of their inability to secure religious rights that would allow them to spend these holidays at home. Holding a graduation on Friday evening was in conflict with Sabbath practices. Berrol notes that "observant teachers and students did not attend, but the schools remained open. There were penalties for the stay-at-homes. Students with otherwise perfect attendance records were denied a much valued certificate upon graduation, and teachers did not get paid for the days that they were absent."[34]

Starting in the 1920s, a struggle was waged by the Jewish community to have the Jewish holidays recognized by the school board. However, while sporadic victories were won on an ad hoc basis, it was only during the 1960s that the board, under pressure from Jewish constituents, finally fixed the problem. A practical problem was created and a permanent solution needed to be found. According to a former teacher of Jewish descent who was part of that struggle, the problem arose during the post-World War II era with the relaxing of housing discrimination laws and the overturning of restrictive covenant clauses in housing developments as unconstitutional, which led to Jewish migration to the suburbs. A sizable number of teachers and secretaries were Jews, and they were now reluctant to travel to the city for classes on Jewish holidays. Although before this time many Jewish students stayed away from school on Jewish holidays, that practice did not lead to school closings on Jewish holidays. According to an informant, a retired teacher who participated in the school system's initial boycott on Jewish holidays, the absence of teachers was the key problem that brought about this change in the institutional operation of the board.

Deana, who is Jewish and now lives in Northern California, reminisces about her school days in New York in the 1960s:

> We didn't go to school, and, I think – we lived in different places. When we lived in Queens, I think the school might have been closed Rosh Hashanah and Yom Kippur. When we lived in the Bronx – when I was talking about how it was mixed, like half and half – there, kids did go to school, but I remember there'd be like five kids who would go to school that day, and they didn't do anything. But they didn't close the schools in the Bronx. It's just that, since most of the kids were Jewish, it was like a day you go to school and play, because they couldn't do anything, because most of the kids weren't there.

In 1960, when the Board of Education prepared the school calendar for 1961–62, closing schools on such Jewish holidays as Rosh Hashanah (two days), Yom Kippur (one day), and the first two days of Passover was mentioned for the first time.[35] Thereafter, every year, whenever it is possible, Jewish High Holidays have been welcomed with the closing of schools. Table 5.1 shows the implementation of this policy for the school years 1999–2000 and 2000–01.

This policy also has been adopted by the City University of New York, as shown in Table 5.2.

Table 5.1 Scheduled school closings for school years 1999–2000 and 2000–01

Fall 1999	Holiday	Spring 2000	Holiday
Mon., Sep 6	Labor Day	Mon., Jan. 17	MLK Jr. Birthday
Mon., Sep 20	**Yom Kippur**	Mon., Feb. 21–Fri., Feb. 25	Midwinter Recess (including Washington's Birthday)
Mon., Oct 11	Columbus Day (observed)		
Tues., Nov 2	Election Day	Thurs., April 20–Fri., April 28	Spring Recess (including Good Friday, Easter, and **Passover**)
Thurs, Nov 11	Veterans Day		
Thurs., Nov. 25–Fri., Nov. 26	Thanksgiving Recess	Mon., May 29,	Memorial Day (observed)
Mon., Dec. 24–Fri., Dec. 31	Winter Recess (including Christmas and New Years)	Thurs., June 8	Anniversary Day (Brooklyn and Queens)
Fall 2000	Holiday	Spring 2001	Holiday
Mon., Sept. 4	Labor Day	Mon., Jan. 15	MLK Jr. Birthday
Mon., Oct. 9	**Yom Kippur** & Columbus Day (observed)	Mon., Feb. 19–Fri., Feb. 23	Midwinter Recess (including Washington's Birthday)
Tues., Nov. 2	Election Day	Thurs., April 9–Fri., April 13	Spring Recess (including Good Friday, Easter, and **Passover**)
Thurs., Nov. 23–Fri., Nov. 24	Thanksgiving Recess Winter Recess (including Christmas and New Years)		
Mon., Dec. 25–Mon., Jan. 1		Mon., May 28	Memorial Day (observed)
		Thurs., June 7	Anniversary Day (Brooklyn and Queens)

Table 5.2 Mainstream and ethnic holidays at CUNY, Fall 1999

Fall 1999	Holiday
Mon., Sept. 6	Labor Day: college closed
Fri., Sept. 10	Only classes scheduled to end before 4:00 will be held
Sat., Sept. 11–Sun., Sept. 12	**Rosh Hashanah: no classes**
Mon., Sept. 20	**Yom Kippur: no classes**
Tues., Sept. 21	Classes to follow a Monday schedule
Mon., Oct. 11	Columbus Day: college closed
Thurs., Nov. 25–Fri., Nov. 26	Thanksgiving: college closed
Mon., Dec. 24	Winter Recess begins
Fri., Dec. 31–Mon., Jan. 3	New Years Day: college closed

Although the school system in New York has made great strides toward recognizing the Jewish High Holidays, the rest of the country is still behind. For example, in the San Francisco Bay Area, the schools allow some kind of tolerance by permitting students to take the day off, but they do not close down for the day. This means that the Jewish students are at the losing end if they do not show up:

This was a conflict. When you went to high school, you didn't want to miss school, because there's such a small Jewish population where we lived, in Santa Rosa, that hardly any kids missed school. So there were maybe one or two kids in your class who would miss school, school would go on as usual, and you didn't want to miss something, or have a report due that day, or have a test, an important test. And I remember, I tried to talk to the school about it, and I really didn't get that much response. And then I went to, there was an organization, called, oh, I can't remember what it was called, but it was like a liaison between the Jewish community and the schools. And they provided the local public schools with Jewish calendars, so the schools would know when the major Jewish holidays were, where kids were going to be out, to try not to schedule tests, or things due. But I know when kids get older, you know, where we live now a lot of kids start wanting to go to school cause they're afraid they're going to miss something, cause school does go on. You know, I don't know what Bob [my son] will do. He may want to go to school.

Thus, the size or strength of the ethnic student and teacher population, which is a reflection of the demography of the group, aided
by a tolerant social climate, are both major factors in determining
whether or not a diaspora imposes its temporality on the local
population by influencing the calendar of its school system. It
remains to be seen whether, in New York City, for example, the
Board of Education will be able to accommodate Muslim students as
well, both recent immigrants and the brethren of the Nation of
Islam. It must be stressed that these changes were made to accommodate the holy days, and not the secular holidays of a diasporic
community.

What is instructive about the closing of schools on Jewish holidays
in New York is that it sheds light on the way the diaspora inverts the
time of the mainstream. It is one of the rare occasions when the
homeland time becomes the dominant local time for individuals
who do not belong to that diasporic group. Global linkage is able to
amplify locally its globality, and that expansion can affect the total
spectrum of the student population, regardless of faith or ethnic
origin. Willingly or not, these other populations are taken in the
flow of the homeland's global temporality, which helps strengthen
its diasporic basis and identity, as well. Because of phenomena like
these, local urban cultures are going through new phases of hybridization whereby syncretism is not a local interaction, but rather a
transnational one. It involves an interaction with a localized
diaspora that is itself in interaction with its homeland.

Ethnic holidays and alternate-side-of-the-street parking regulations

Another way to evaluate the accommodation of ethnic holidays by
mainstream institutions is to examine whether local governments
continue or suspend their normal, day-to-day operations. It has been
a long-standing tradition in New York to implement alternate-side-
of-the-street parking as a way to sweep and keep the streets clean.
For many years, alternate-side-of-the-street parking was suspended
only on legal and some Christian holidays, such as Christmas. Little
attention was paid to the need of other faiths. Now, with a greater
awareness and sensitivity to ethnic holidays, some of them have been
incorporated into the schedules for the suspension of alternate-side-

of-the-street parking. Major Jewish and Muslim holidays are honored in this way (see Table 5.3).

Ethnics accomplish victories such as this when the city imposes regulations on the entire population to facilitate matters for one group of people. Although such groups may have their strengths in specific neighborhoods, these regulations affect not only their neighborhoods, but the entire city. These ethnic holy days are not recognized as state or city holidays, but simply as special days when alternate-side-of-the-street parking is suspended. In alternate-side-of-the-street parking regulations and accommodations of a similar type, we find the first level of recognition of these ethnic holidays by the city. It is sectoral recognition: It affects street parking – or the school system – but does not directly affect on other aspects of the city's social life.

In New York City only Christians, Jews, and Muslims have been successful in convincing the city government to suspend the applications of the alternate-side parking rules on some of their holidays. Other groups have attempted to have such privileges extended to their ethnic holidays as well, but so far to no avail. For example, the *New York Times* reported on April 18, 1998 that " a City Council committee pushed yesterday to make the Chinese New Year the 31st holiday on which alternate-side parking rules are suspended, but officials of the Giuliani administration argued that the proposal would mean dirtier streets."

Subaltern citizens and hegemonic holidays

While the power of demographics has allowed some ethnic groups to achieve at least the first level of recognition for their ethnic holidays, it is more frequently the case that the holidays of the hegemonic temporality have exerted an effect on such ethnic events, either maximizing or muting their importance, sometimes reconstituting the ethnic holiday within the hegemonic one and modifying its meaning.

The proximity of an ethnic holiday to a state holiday or Christian holiday makes it more visible. Sometimes the ethnic holiday appropriates the characteristics of such a hegemonic holiday, and sometimes the proximity simply lessens its visibility. Hanukah has become a more elaborate ritual because of its proximity to Christmas. One can also think of the relations of Good Friday to Passover. According

Table 5.3 Alternate-side-of-the-street parking regulations

1999	Holiday	1999	Holiday
Fri, Jan 1	New Year's Day	Mon, May 31	Memorial Day (observed)
Mon, Jan 18	Martin Luther King Jr's Birthday	Sun., July 4	Independence Day
Mon, Jan 18	**Idul Fitr: First Day**	Mon., July 5	Independence Day (observed)
Tues, Jan 19	**Idul Fitr: Second Day**	Sun, Aug. 15	Assumption of the Blessed Virgin
Wed, Jan 20	**Idul Fitr: Third Day**	Mon., Sept. 6	Labor Day
Fri, Feb 12	Lincoln's Birthday	Sat, Sept. 11	**Rosh Hashanah: First Day**
Mon, Feb 15	Washington's Birthday (observed)	Sun., Sept. 12	**Rosh Hashanah: Second Day**
Sun, March 28	**Idul-Adha: First Day**	Mon., Sept. 20	**Yom Kippur**
Mon, March 29	**Idul-Adha: Second Day**	Sat., Sept. 25	**Succoth: First Day**
Tues, March 30	**Idul-Adha: Third Day**	Sun., Sept. 26	**Succoth: Second Day**
Thurs, April 1	Holy Thursday	Sat., Oct. 2	**Shimini Atzereth**
Thurs, April 1	**Passover: First Day**	Sun., Oct. 11	**Simchas Torah**
Fri, April 2	**Passover: Second Day**	Mon., Oct. 11	Columbus Day
Fri, April 2	Good Friday	Mon., Nov. 1	All Saints Day
Wed, April 7	**Passover: Seventh Day**	Tues., Nov. 2	Election Day
Thurs, April 8	**Passover: Eighth Day**	Thurs., Nov. 11	Veterans Day
Thurs, April 8	Holy Thursday (Orthodox)	Thurs., Nov. 25	Thanksgiving Day
Fri, April 9	Good Friday (Orthodox)	Wed., Dec. 8	Immaculate Conception
Thurs, May 13	Solemnity of Ascension	Fri., Dec. 24	Christmas Day (observed)
Fri, May 21	**Shavuot: First Day**	Sat., Dec. 25	Christmas Day
Sat, May 22	**Shavuot: Second Day**	Fri., Dec. 31	New Year's Eve

to the school calendar in New York City, students are given off the first two days of Passover only if Good Friday is one of those days. When Passover falls outside the Christian holy week, only the first day of Passover is a school holiday.

The dominant holiday affects the social life of the subaltern as it disrupts their routine. As we have seen, some celebrate it in form, if not in spirit, by exchanging gifts. Others escape the aura of the day by moving temporarily to areas where they are not bombarded by television ads for such festivities. A Jewish informant told me that the family prefers to take its vacation around Christmas time. Others stay put and develop alternative ways to cope with this temporal disjuncture. For example, one Jewish family told me that because the country is at a standstill, they cannot ignore these mainstream holidays and must work their way around them.

> On Christmas, we usually try to go to a Chinese restaurant, because we know it's going to be open. And the movies aren't too crowded. And you got to do something. Everything's closed on Christmas, you got to find something to do. So one year we did go to, like a soup kitchen, and served, you know, Christmas dinner.
>
> It's hard, though, I remember working in the office at Hewlett Packard at Christmas, you know, because they'd always have these, you know, big Christmas decorations up and I felt kind of like I wasn't part of that or it wasn't for me. There was a time I was feeling very sensitive about it, and that – I felt like it was mixing religion, you know, with school and work, and public stuff. Now I see it more as like a consumer holiday. I mean, it really is. I don't think most people who celebrate Christmas celebrate it as a religious holiday. Which is kind of sad in a way.

In general, mainstream holidays are literally imposed on the population, while the subaltern holidays are simply tolerated and the participants accommodated. In the celebration of ethnic holidays, the hegemonic system occasionally bends its rules a little so as to accommodate the ethnics. Ethnic minority students may be exempt from classes if they have a religious holiday, but this is not necessarily imposed on the rest of the class.

The subaltern status of ethnic holidays cannot be explained solely in terms of ethnicity or race, because some European immigrant groups confront a similar situation. Their ethnicity does not allocate their temporal practices a spot on the dominant social space of the hegemonic community. In this sense, they are treated like other minorities, despite their apparent racial identity with the dominant group. In its January 7, 1999 edition, the *Los Angeles Times* reports that "unlike December 25, the date observed by Western churches, Orthodox Christmas is not a legal holiday. Some Orthodox Christians must choose between attending church and showing up for work or going to school." So the dominant race is not always located in the dominant festive space. At times it shares the subaltern space with the subaltern races. This highlights the diversity of temporal status within the Euro-American group itself.

By and large, some of the mainstream holidays such as Thanksgiving do not mean much to ethnic communities and are sites in which they are made to experience their subalternization. In other words, they are made to celebrate imposed holidays whose significance and rituals do not mean much to them. The ethnics use these forced holidays for other purposes.

Appropriation of ethnic holidays by the mainstream

The most thoroughgoing effect of the hegemonic temporality on subaltern ethnic holidays is, of course, their appropriation by the mainstream. Usually, the mainstream plays a marginal role in the performance of ethnic holidays, more as observers than as actors. In fact, some of these holidays invite the observation of the mainstream community, such as Chinese New Year, and holidays such as the Saint Patrick Day parade, which is a magnet for attention-hungry local politicians. In cases such as these, the mainstream assists the ethnics in the carrying of their holiday celebrations, providing logistical advice and police protection. In rare cases, however, the mainstream appropriates the ethnic holiday and turns it into its own. This does not happen because of the strength of the population of the minority group, or because that group has somehow imposed its will on the majority. Nor is it a matter of co-optation by the members of the hegemonic temporality as a way of neutralizing the minority group. Instead, it usually serves the immediate interests of at least some major faction of the majority.

During the hearings that led to the impeachment of President Clinton, for example, some members of Congress, with the help of a group of rabbis in Washington, DC and New York, castigated their Republican colleagues for their lack of respect for the Jewish High Holy Days: When "The Republican-controlled House Judiciary Committee voted along party lines today to release the videotape of President Clinton's grand jury testimony, along with 2,800 pages of documents from the inquiry into his relationship with Monica Lewinsky . . . Several members of Congress protested the decision to make the material public on the Jewish New Year."[36]

Perhaps the first case of such an appropriation in US history was not so much an appropriation from an ethnic other as a premature gesture toward globalization in the name of the Rights of Man: the appropriation of the holidays of the French Revolution by the American mainstream community during the administration of George Washington:

> In New York City the celebrations of Bastille Day in 1793 were extensive enough to prompt the cancellation of classes at Columbia College on Monday July 15, while on Sunday July 14 the Presbyterians of Princeton feasted and drank toasts, held a celebratory ball at which both men and women gave toasts and sang the "Marseillaise." . . . For such a community this was a remarkably large-scale celebration, and was one which would have commanded the attention of most if not all of the community's residents.[37]

Such popular celebrations were a sign of the support of the American public for the success of the French Revolution. Newman shows that these festive events were concocted mostly by members of the fledgling political party known as the Democratic Republicans (eventually known simply as the Democrats) and took place mostly in the Northern states. The intent of these mainstream revelers was partisan – "to register their particular opposition to Federalist policies and personnel."[38] Celebrations of the French Revolution thus furnished "impoverished white men, white women of all classes, and black men and women with far greater opportunities for participation in popular politics than were afforded by domestic festive occasions."[39]

The fact that such an appropriation of these French holidays did not last long is a testament to the difficulty of deminoritizing and majoritizing holidays that are not already part of the mainstream. Because they reflect the singularity of a different history and because the mainstream may not be familiar or care about this specific history, it is likely that ethnic holidays will continue to be celebrated mostly by the members of the group who have a vested interest to keep alive the memory of the event so that they may reconnect to that tradition and transmit diasporic culture to the youngsters. However, the practice of multiculturalism requires equity in the recognition of such temporal practices, and it is likely that diasporic communities will continue to fight so that the same privileges extended to mainstream holidays may be extended to ethnic holidays in order to desubalternize the temporal means through which their identities are expressed.

Transnational temporality

As we have seen in the transglobalized temporalities of the Jewish and Muslim weeks, transnational temporality also finds local expression in the celebration of ethnic holidays, operating through an infrastructure of translocal sites. This infrastructure makes possible the relations among various sites in the network and between the homeland and the diaspora. Globalization implodes the structure of these festive events because they are nodes in a network of transnational temporal flows, and, as such, are expressed as points of juncture where the global displays its local face. This globalization process tends to be articulated unevenly at the local level, feeding some sectors more than others, depending on the logic that is heralded.[40] Temporal difference is detected at the point of inscription of the global in the local, in the articulation of the social structure, and the hierarchy of positions that may result. The unevenness that results from the implosion of globalization explains the existence of heterogeneous temporal sites inside the global network of relations.

Diverse means are used and reasons invoked to maintain or intensify transnational relations during that period of ethnic festivities. The ethnic holidays are an occasion for the renewal of relationships with the homeland because of family obligations, for the purpose of engaging in economic transactions, or simply to keep alive the channels of transnational politics. Ethnic media (television, radio, and Web pages) broadcast the festivities in the homeland in direct transmission to the diaspora, as in the case of the speech from the throne by the president to the transnation or some powerful homily delivered by an imam. Other means used to intensify or maintain transnational relations are visits by government officials to the diasporic community to report on what the government is doing, fund raising by members of the diaspora to pay for local projects by the nongovernmental organizations or religious institutions that they support, the organization of special events by consular offices to celebrate these ethnic holidays with the participation of members of the diaspora, visits of diasporic members to the homeland to be part of the national festivities there, and dependence on the homeland for the calculation of prayer times and the beginning and ending of holy days and national holidays.

Foreign missions close their offices on national holidays of the country of origin and on the national holidays of the country of residence. Here is an instance where the mixing of the homeland time with the hegemonic time is accomplished on a daily basis – homeland time for the purpose of communicating with the original nation, and hegemonic time for the purpose of dealing with the public in the country of residence.

The role of the foreign consulate or embassy is strategic in fostering the celebration of diasporic holidays. While the purpose may be to invite host-country guests, diasporans are also invited so that these guests may meet them, foster friendship between the two nations, and maintain a relationship between the diaspora and the homeland. The organization of such an event is a matter of maintaining the unity of the group, projecting a positive side of the government to the diaspora, enlisting the aid of the diaspora for the continued success of government projects, or enticing the diaspora to lobby a foreign government on behalf of the national government. The participation of foreign missions in the organization of such celebratory events is not peculiar only to the United States. James[41] found that the Philippine Embassy in Lagos organized independence parties to which both the Filipino community and guests from the host country were invited.

Sometimes the government goes one step further by inviting members of the diaspora to visit the homeland as special guests of the national government. "The personal invitation of some individual immigrants or representatives of Arab organizations in the US to visit their original countries is one such official link. These invitations usually take place on occasions celebrating national holidays; for example, since the revolution in Iraq on July 14, 1958, the government regularly invites representatives from the Iraqi community in Detroit to attend the celebration of this occasion."[42] The homeland government may even send a delegation to meet with members of the diaspora to discuss matters of common concern. "Visits by government officials to the Arab community in this country are another official link. Occasionally different Arab governments send special delegates to tour the communities of their respective nationalities to meet with them and discuss issues of common concern."[43]

At times, institutions such as mosques within the diaspora itself organize formal means to activate contact with the homeland. "On occasions, these religious institutions organize a chartered plane to enable members to visit their original homes and to renew their ties with the homeland."[44]

Because holidays revive the intensity of transnational relations, they are an occasion to inject in the diaspora a good dose of homeland cultural ways while also providing an opportunity for the diaspora to influence the ways of the homeland. The relations between the diaspora and the homeland thus are not between two fixed points, but rather between two evolving sites that influence each other because of the linkages that tie them to each other.

I was told by an imam that the Islamic Cultural Center in New York City occasionally invites Islamic scholars from Egypt to spend the month of Ramadan and lecture to the community. These scholars help maintain the oneness of Islam and reinvigorate the community with a good dose of homeland traditions of interpretation. In a sense, one may say that "these churches and mosques function as important transnational links tying Arab communities here to the Arab world and reinforcing traditional values of the old country and preserving ethnic identity."[45]

The analysis of diasporic new years and holidays helps us to understand the hybridity of the globalization process as it expresses itself in a hegemonic form in some sites and in a subjugated form in others. As we observed in the study of the different weekly diasporic temporalities, the malleability of the global temporal flows seems to depend on local conditions that shape their local outcomes without changing the global nature of the process itself.

The global time of ethnic holidays also provides us a lens through which we can once again see how the architecture of global temporal flows is hierarchized. Diasporic holidays are manifestly globalized local temporal events because they serve as nodal points for transnational relations, because their occurrence inside a global calendrical system links their temporality to that of the homeland, because their global meanings serve as offshoot celebrations of homeland holidays, and because their origins must be sought in the homeland and provide the rationale for such celebrations.

Global time, in its local expression, tends to suggest that locality should not be conceived of as a fixed reality, but may perhaps be conceptualized as an entity in motion.[46] The space of flows and the time of flows are two main elements that characterize the identity of the local site as enmeshed in the globalization process. Ethnic holidays, because they are located inside the time of flows, emerge as singular sites that reflect at the local level the global flows of time. The "space of flows"[47] corresponds to the time of flows in reference to the globalization of local sites. By "time of flows," I mean the process by which duration traverses localities, reshapes them, reorients them in diverse directions, pluralizes their structures, and relocates them as nodes in transglobal networks. The ethnic holiday is yet another temporal site in which the time of flows expresses itself through crisscrossing border practices – through the dominance of its globality over its locality. In fact, such holidays make sense to the extent that one can connect them to an extraterritorial site, that is, to the primitive event that ushered their birth in the homeland.

As with the other transglobalized temporalities we have examined, it is probably more accurate to speak of a multiplicity of globalities, because the transnational temporal currents they generate display different logics, pursue different goals, and aim at different outcomes.[48] Muslim holidays anchor the diasporic communities in a global process that differs much from the celebrations of Bastille Day by French revelers in eighteenth-century New York.[49] For the former, the purpose is religious and obligatory, while for the latter, it is secular and political.

The globalization process thus does not produce a homogeneous world, but rather generates local sites that continue to differ from one another.[50] This is made possible because global time is expressed locally and is shaped by local conditions. Diasporic holidays are a vivid expression of the manner in which localities play a role in their deployment as outposts and extensions of homeland time. The heterogeneity of practices rhythms the choreography of the globalization of temporality.

Conclusion: Chronopolis
and Metropolis

Multiculturalism implies the Balkanization of diversity; spatial, religious, linguistic, racial, or temporal segregation; the homogeneity of ethnic groups so that they can be differentiated from one another in the name of cultural authenticity; and the presumed ethnic interaction that must go on to express the civic identity of the local community.[1] Furthermore, it presupposes that the interaction is equal, carried out in a horizontal plane, instead of in a hierarchical axis between a dominant and dominated groups in which it is power that is the prevalent mechanism shaping the relationship.

Charles Taylor's notion of the "politics of recognition" must be seen as a top-down approach to the issue of multiculturalism because it still implies the freezing of difference and the legitimization of minority status by the majority.[2] Multiculturalism understood from the bottom up is a much more radical project that implies the insertion of the ethnic group as an equal entity inside the constitutional project of society. It projects an equality of membership without condescension as part of the definition of the democratic project. In the process, it is citizenship, not race, that becomes the principal criterion that counts in the allocation of "status."

Although national origin remains in the background for those who wish to use such a factor in the performance of their identity, different temporalities based on religious traditions will continue to be part of the working of democracy, because they allow the necessary freedom to perform and celebrate the "time of difference" as a complement to the "space of difference." Time is a factor of difference in that it is used as a criterion to stratify a multicultural system.

This study of New York City, through an analysis of diasporic temporalities in their relation to the mainstream community and the homeland, provides a productive point of view for decoding the urban multiculturalism of the metropolis. Throughout the book, I have argued that the interaction between the dominant and subaltern temporalities is wholly mediated by crisscrossing global flows that are constitutive of the local scene. The dominant temporality is not a fixed site, but is remolded from below because of its relations with these diasporic temporalities. Diasporic temporalities are, likewise, constantly being reshaped as a result of their adjustment to the ways of the hegemonic temporal regime. To understand how the situation has come into being, I will attempt to specify its genealogy by locating the production of the local process in the context of the relations of diasporic temporalities with the mainstream system and the homeland, including other extraterritorial sites.

Mainstream/subaltern temporal relations

The politics of mainstream time *vis-à-vis* the subaltern has not remained the same throughout the years. It has evolved from a hostile stance to more or less theoretical acceptance of diversity to the extent that such a practice does not undermine the hegemony of the mainstream system. The struggle of the so-called ethnic minorities cannot be fought only in the political and economic realm, however, but must also be carried out in the temporal realm, since multiculturalism implies the emancipation of diasporic temporalities, as well.

The politics of mainstream society correlates well with its spatial politics and its temporal practices *vis-à-vis* minoritized groups. They are part of the same politics used by the mainstream to maintain hegemony, readjusted to meet the social conditions of specific periods. The first phase of the relationship between the dominant group and less politically and economically powerful groups was geared toward the exclusion of nonwhites by harassing, persecuting, and criminalizing their practices. The interest was a local one, that of subjugating and exploiting, if possible, the group in order to prevent it from competing – on an equal footing – with the mainstream for hegemony. Similar practices were deemed to be legal for whites and illegal for nonwhites. The process of the criminalization of minorities worked on two levels: the criminalizing of their temporal religious practices, which were not confined to Sunday, and the criminalizing of their secular practices, which were undertaken in tandem with whites. For example, one reads in the Sunday laws established in 1695 in New York that "it was lawful to travel any distance under twenty miles, for the purpose of attending public worship. It was also lawful to 'go for a physician or nurse.' These exemptions were not good in favor of unchristianized Indians."[3] The exclusion was racial, since most Native Americans at that time were yet to be converted to Christianity. The exceptions to the rules covered both Christian and non-Christian whites. To impose its time, the mainstream used the law to regulate the time of the other in order to subjugate it.

The second phase of that relationship was geared toward a process of segregated assimilation. This shift came about with the ratification of the Constitution, which placed all residents inside an "imagined national community" with the caveat that inclusion for nonwhites would occur through marginalization at the bottom of society. The new politics of time recognized the legal rights of non-Christians to worship on a day specified by their own ethnic temporalities, but also prevented non-Christians from working on Sunday, thereby forcing them to abide by the mainstream day of worship. The blue laws of 1885 for New York City recognized the right of non-Christians to worship on their respective day, but kept it as an exception. This would protect them from "prosecution," but not from "arrest."[4] The harassment factor thus was not eliminated from the law. Non-Christians were still placed at a disadvantage because of the discrimination embedded in the blue laws.

The policy of segregated assimilation did not work well in the area of schooling. For example, the absence of non-Christian students on their respective holy days did not impel the city to close the schools on those days. Quite the contrary. Schissel, alluding to his own experience in New York, remembers that "I was one of a few Jewish students in my public school in the 1930s, and I recall that some teachers regularly scheduled important tests on Jewish holidays."[5] Doubtless, such an effort was expanded to entice the students to join the practices of the mainstream community as part of an assimilation scheme.

The third phase was one of accommodation, geared toward the

recognition of ethnic time as part of the general policy of celebrating the diversity of ethnic heritages. This phase did not recognize ethnic parity, but rather plurality. Ethnic time was not seen as equal to mainstream time, but was regarded as contributing to the success of American life. In some states, such a policy coincided with the repeals of Sunday laws. In this accommodation phase, the state established procedures for facilitating such matters. But it remained clear that these were procedural gains, and mainstream time was still hegemonic. This accommodation went as far as to introduce ethnic time into the planning of city events and to legitimate the ethnic definition of the day so as to accommodate members' needs in the area of religious, educational, and ludic activities.

In schools, this new policy simply accommodated ethnic students without addressing the problem of inequality. We are told, for example, that "in a concession to Jewish parents, the board recommended that on the High Holy Days, teachers not give tests or introduce new material."[6] This laissez-faire policy created a new set of problems for all involved. Schools remained open on ethnic holidays, and some ethnic parents kept their children at home on such days, preventing the school from functioning properly.

The last phase, the phase that we are in at present – the multicultural phase – is a major shift from the preceding phases. The three preceding phases concerned themselves with defining the status of the subaltern other within the state. In contrast, the multicultural phase is multinational. It goes beyond the boundaries of the nation-state, opens up the system, establishes transnational connections, and thereby reinvigorates their temporal practices and prevents the mainstream hegemony from incarcerating or ghettoizing ethnic practices. The shift here is from ethnicization to diasporization, because the connections with the homeland as an anchor reproduce the vitality of these practices. This phase has rearranged the relations of the mainstream with the temporalities of the ethnics: sometimes to cultivate good relations, sometimes for foreign policy purposes, and sometimes to exploit this burgeoning market or clientele commercially.

In the multicultural phase, provisions have been made to close schools on some ethnic holidays. In 1999, the Paterson School Board in New Jersey was the only one that closed its schools on the two holiest Muslim days, Eid al-Fitr and Eid al-adha. Muslim parents were asking for equality in the way the school handles ethnic holidays. Until then, their only alternative was to pull their children out of school for these two days while the school continued business as usual. The new policy reflects their wishes to have "their children home on those two holy days without missing schoolwork."[7] A similar treatment was conferred on the Jewish holidays in some districts. For example, it was reported that "in Montgomery [Virginia], where more than half of the estimated 165,000 Jews in the Washington area live, schools will be closed September 6 for Rosh Hashanah."[8]

The closing of schools for some Jewish and Muslim holy days and not for other holy days has created a level of tension in some communities. It seems as if some ethnic groups are favored over others, thereby hierarchizing the position of groups within the minority category. This demonstrates how complex a policy of multiculturalism can be if every group is asking for its fair share of holidays. Will there be enough days left for schooling?

In various ways, the ethnic temporalities affect the mainstream sector of society in this new multicultural temporal regime. As we have seen throughout, perhaps the most visible interface is the relationship of ethnic temporalities with the business sector and the municipal government. Business pays attention to some ethnic calendrical events in order to exploit them for commercial publicity. This is evident when a firm publicizes its products on a parade float or concocts a specific advertisement for the occasion during a local mainstream or ethnic television program. Sometimes the same advertisement may be repeated in places where the ethnic population has some demographic strengths, including the homeland. For example, the *Wall Street Journal* reported in the February 15, 1996 edition that "Coca-Cola will launch its first global TV commercial pegged to Lunar New Year next week, featuring a gigantic dragon festooned with 6200 Coca-Cola cans."[9] Politicians participate in these holiday events (parades, festivals, church services) for the purpose of enhancing their popularity among this segment of society and to beg for votes on election day. In its October 10, 1988 edition, the *New York Times* reported that "Mr. Bush, campaigning like a local politician seeking local office, joined in the annual Houby Day Parade that went through Cicero and Berwyn, two suburban Chicago communities with large immigrant populations from Eastern Europe . . . Mr. Bush rode in a red fire engine and waved energetically at thousands of onlookers along the mile-long route of the parade for Houby Day, an event that began as a Czech celebration of the mushroom harvest." Some of these holidays would probably be less known if it were not for the recognition they enjoy from mainstream business and political figures.

Because of the transnational relations it engenders, globalization makes it more difficult to manage the plurality of temporalities inside the American city because the city government no longer has the monopoly over the public deployment or expression of these temporalities. As Shain has argued,[10] relations with the homeland and external factors complicate the grammatical rules of the performance of multiculturalism. Relations with the homeland have strengthened the ethnic position of some groups in the American landscape. The performance of these temporalities is reinforced by these external linkages, which further justifies the existence of such temporalities for the city government. Transnational temporalities express the transglobal infrastructure of the American city.

Temporal ghettos

One thinks of the ghetto as a spatial enclosure brought about by racial segregation or religious exclusion – the incarceration of a group inside a delimited area and its isolation from the rest of society. The ghetto concept primarily evokes territorial space, but since calendrical time is also an aspect that separates an ethnic or religious group from the dominant system of society, one is justified in speaking of temporal ghettos. In this sense, New York City as a metropolis is made up of spatial ghettos like Harlem and temporal ghettos like the Jewish and Muslim chronopolises, with their multiple sites of incorporation and residence in the city. Territorial concentration is the cornerstone of spatial ghettos. However, concentration is not a tangible variable that characterizes the identity of the chronopolises. Temporal ghettos exist even in conditions of geographical dispersion of the population. They share the same calendar in the reckoning of time, they migrate from their calendar to the Western calendar to participate in the working of civil society, and they return to their temporalities to mark religious rituals and to accomplish acts of personal piety.

A "temporal ghetto" is a community that upholds its cultural practices according to a duration principle, on rhythms and cadences based on a calendrical system different from that of the mainstream. As we have seen, the deghettoization of their ethnic temporalities is a project of some ethnic groups as they struggle to emancipate and hegemonize their subalternized and minoritized communities.

Border time

Analysis of the behavior of the chronopolis leads to the understanding that it is the expression of border time in two important ways. First, the chronopolis is a public expression of hybrid time, the site resulting from the meeting of the local with the global. The chronopolis is neither the pure reflection of the homeland time nor the pure assimilation of mainstream American time, but rather a syncretistic outcome that combines elements from both. As a routine, such a reconstituted time provides a balance where individuals can partake in both mainstream and ethnic activities. Ethnic time is prioritized for religious obligations and national festive celebrations, while the mainstream time takes over for secular functions and official holidays. While spatial ghettoization means complete separation between the mainstream and the ethnic group in matters related to housing, temporally segregated ghettos imply a sectoral and more fluid type of separation.

To put the point another way, the chronopolis is located between the mainstream and the homeland. It sees itself as a tentacle of the homeland, but not a pure copy of it. The chronopolis engages in a continuing negotiation with the mainstream for the recognition of the temporal difference that sustains its cultural difference. Betwixt and between the mainstream and the homeland, the chronopolis gains constant input from the homeland through transnational migration and bidirectional border-crossing practices. In this way, the changing modulation of the rhythmic time of the homeland feeds and reshapes the chronopolis. I have in mind the addition of new holidays, the transfer of celebrations from one day to another for practical reasons, or the upgrading, downgrading, and disappearance of holidays. One may think of holidays created by a government to improve its nationalist image that were eliminated by a new regime with a different state agenda. Because of the dependence of the chronopolis for the justification of such holidays, changes in the scheduling or the elimination or addition of holidays in the homeland would result in change in the ethnopolis.

Thus, we can see that the chronopolis does not have control over the deployment of its calendrical time. This calendar depends on the ebb and flow of the homeland time, and, as such, it is vulnerable to these global occurrences. Border time must also be seen in terms of the dependence of the ethnopolis for both the organization and the practice of its temporal life. Although they live in diaspora, the diasporans are still under the normative regime and tradition of the homeland. The calendar manifests cultural temporal continuity and symbolizes the globalization of the homeland by way of temporal expansion.

Those who live in the social margins of the chronopolis illustrate the second way in which, the chronopolis is the expression of border time. These are individuals who, due to their ethnicity, could blend with the temporalities of the chronopolis, but do not do so for their own personal reasons. They are not assimilated with the temporality of the mainstream, either, because they lack the cultural inclination to do so. They do not fit in either site, but are located at the borders between them. They thus define the border by their transgressions of it. This condition is more ambiguous than that of people who are located in the ethnopolis or the mainstream. It may be the product of a transitional period in someone's life that is resolved in one way or the other, or it can be a permanent condition in which one utilizes the best from each side in order to define a life of one's own. This is reminiscent of the conditions of those locked in the spatial border of American ghettos. In contrast to border time, border space reflects the conditions of individuals caught against their will in such a structural position. Much is known about the spatial ghettos, however very little is known about their borders – spatial and temporal.

In either case, border time refers to individuals who live in the interstices of both calendars, Gregorian and native. They negotiate both without being confined by either one of them. This category is different from the practices of those who primarily use one calendar while making sporadic use of the other.

Ethnic calendars

As we have seen, a common sight in the diasporic community is the visible presence and use of the ethnic calendar. These appear in three different formats, depending on the institution that prepares, prints, and distributes them. The basic calendar that circulates among well-established groups such as the Chinese and Jews is not different in its organization and layout from the mainstream American calendar and is for all intents and purposes a double calendar. It provides double dates for each day: the Gregorian and the diasporic, a double month for each month, and a double year for each year. In such a calendar, one may follow the deployment of the day, week, month, and year according to the lunar, lunisolar, or solar system of time reckoning. Since these different months and years do not have the same length, the day dates are not identical. As a general rule, the beginning and end of the month or the year also do not coincide. For example, Saturday, January 1, 2000 corresponded in the Jewish calendar to Sabbath day 23 Tevet (month), 5760 (year), and in the Muslim calendar to 24 Ramadan, 1420 (year). Since the beginning of the month or the year in the ethnic or pan-ethnic calendar seldom coincides with the beginning of the month and the year in the Gregorian calendar, but always falls before or after, inside the Gregorian month or year there may be located two different months in the Jewish or Muslim calendar and two different years inside the Gregorian year. For example, inside 2000 are included two (incomplete) years of the Muslim calendar 1420 (January–April 5) and 1421 (April 6–December 31) and two (incomplete) years of the Jewish calendar 5760 (January–mid-September) and 5761 (mid-September–December). The mainstream and the ethnic calendar also differ in the ways in which the ethnic holidays are singled out in bold, or in a different color, and the exact time for the opening of the weekly Sabbath that is indicated on the calendar. Because midday or twelve o'clock in the solar-based system does not correspond to midday in the lunar-based system, the Muslim calendar also provides a table of prayer times that accompanies the calendar. In another format, the ethnic calendar is provided as a special bulletin or booklet for the faithful. This form of circulation is used by the mosques and is often done with calculations prepared by the national government. Such a calendar is in circulation for specifically religious purposes. When it appears in a booklet form, some religious commentaries are added concerning the meaning of the fasting that is required from the faithful during the month of Ramadan, for example.

The third format, which is now common among the Muslims, is the addition of the calendar to the last pages of the yellow pages. Such a calendar tends to reflect national sentiments, orientations, and preoccupations. For example, the Muslim calendar is appended to such ethnic yellow pages as *The Iranian Directory* and *The American Muslim Fast Yellow Pages*. Yellow pages editors see it as a service to the community. Since the yellow pages are reference books for business, why not use them as a reference book to access information on prayer times? This is a singular type of service that the mainstream yellow pages does not provide to their patrons and that distinguishes them from some ethnic yellow pages.

Since the ethnics follow the rhythm of the temporality of the homeland, calendars are issued around the ethnic new year. Such calendars are made available to the brethren in synagogues or places of worship and in public places such as day-care centers, restaurants, ethnic businesses, and nonprofit organizations. After the ethnic new year passes, it is more difficult to find them. One of the most popular Jewish calendars distributed in the San Francisco/Silicon Valley metropolitan area is sponsored and financed by Safeway, a food and drug chain store with commercial outlets throughout the western United States. It is adorned with Jewish religious motifs and short commentaries by Rabbi Tzvi Freeman.

The Muslim calendar is issued around Ramadan, irrespective of the national origin of the group. Small variations do exist pertaining to the religious tradition of the group, whether they belong to the Sunni or Shi'ite Muslim membership. The Iranians distribute the Persian calendar around Norouz, their new year, which falls on March 21.

These ethnic calendars use both the ethnic language and American English so that they are accessible to both newcomers and the second generation. The ethnic dates (day date, month, and year) are provided next to the American date. In some calendars, the ethnic date is given prominence over the Gregorian date, and vice versa in other calendars.

The Jewish calendar introduces the year according to the Jewish way of time reckoning, that is, with September as the first month (Tishrei). The calendar contains all the months, from September to

August. However, to make it easier to use, the basic pattern of the American calendar is used. That is, the American month serves as a background.

The ethnic calendar is a referential guide that regulates the life of a segment of the population. It is a deep structure that in a concise way provides the temporal regularity of the homeland in a way that also displays the surface structure of hegemonic temporalities. In this sense, the ethnic calendar is different from the homeland because it also indicates important days – holidays – of the country of adoption. It is syncretistic, but projects its own hegemony over the mainstream calendar. It is one area where the ethnics project their hegemony over the subalternity of the mainstream.

It is also expansive. It sets dates that are also used by non-ethnics because they are invited as guests or friends. In other words, the calendar sporadically affects the lives of the other people, as well – individuals who use the services of the neighborhood and who are made aware of days when such services are not available.

Global infrastructure of diasporic globalization

The transglobal infrastructure of the American city is temporized, hierarchized, multisited, and networked through transnational connectivities. One moves from the notion of time that produces a series of things by way of the human universe it affects, as Thompson has shown in his studies of industrial time, to a conceptualization of time that is itself temporized. In other words, one must also study the temporality of time.

For Held *et al.*, "globalization may be thought of initially as the widening, deepening and speeding up of worldwide interconnectedness in all aspects of contemporary social life."[11] Because of this interconnectedness, territorial boundaries are not an obstacle in the operation of these links. Therefore, a locale can be influenced by a site outside its boundaries. Because globalization is pluridirectional, a site of power may influence a subaltern site the same way that a subaltern site may influence a headquarters site. In the context of a multicultural social formation, one must think of segmented temporal relations. This is a segment of the diaspora that is being influenced by or that influences a segment of the homeland. This differentiation of social relations accounts for the disjuncture and multiplicity of times in the American city.

The relations of the chronopolis with the metropolis are constantly being affected by the relations it maintains with the homeland. Over the years, as part of its incorporation in the structure of the city, the chronopolis adjusts its temporal ways with those of the metropolis. This temporal fusion exerts a continuing pull factor as new elements migrate to the other side through assimilation, so that the units are not completely distinct, but are linked to each other by individuals who belong to both.

The relations of the chronopolis with the homeland produce a double process, reinforcing the chronopolis's posture as a temporal island in a sea of mainstream temporality and disturbing the relations of the chronopolis with mainstream temporality. The reinforcement is done through migration, transnational relations of all kinds, and through the maintenance of the temporal circuit that provides a justification for the existence of that diasporic temporality – a temporality that makes sense only in reference to a homeland. Reinforcement is necessary to prevent cooptation, assimilation, and loss of a distinct temporality that is part of the identity of the diasporic community.

The relations of the chronopolis with the homeland are factors of transnationality that feed the inherent conflict between the mainstream and the chronopolis because they are operating under two different time systems that each have their own rationale or logic. One may speak of a transnational conflict because it implicates the relations of the mainstream with the chronopolis.

Hybridity explains the makeup of the chronopolis. It is not hybrid by fusion, whereby the mainstream meshes with the homeland cultural time in a specific diasporic context. Instead, it is hybrid by conversion. This hybridity is both interstitial and transversal. It is the outcome of its location in the interstices of the mainstream temporality and the process by which it constructs itself. That is, it parallels, penetrates, traverses, and exits mainstream time. This explains how it maintains itself by serving as a local site in a transglobal circuit of interaction.

In framing the local sites that comprise the global architecture of the globalization of time, it is important to remark that these sites have their own configuration because of "the varieties of response to the globalization process."[12] This led Robertson to speak of them as the manifest and emblematic signs of the "localization of globality."[13]

Diverse mechanisms that are part of the architecture of globalization are identified as "space of flows,"[14] the importance of locality as fixed or malleable sites,[15] and as Held *et al.*'s notion of "aterritoriality" borrowed from Badie.[16] As Meyer *et al.*[17] put it, "globalization is not only about flows but also entails constant efforts toward closure and fixing at all levels." New boundaries are created to meet not only the desiderata of the homeland, but also those of the chronopolis. These boundaries are porous because of their location and the very nature of the diasporic community. Their porousness is a reflection of their integration, interaction, and resistance to the mainstream.

Because not all flows are the same, there is a need to differentiate and recognize the unevenness of global temporal flows. Temporal flows are not unidirectional, but are hierarchized, which indicates their unevenness. Such a hierarchy expresses their stratification in terms of importance and sectoral connections. This is why their sectoral effect on the ground may be uneven.[18] Kelly speaks of "asymmetries in global flows."[19] Homelands with diasporic settlements have developed "global chronopolitics"[20] that allow them to influence, expand, and shape the direction of diasporic temporalities.

There are at least two types of temporal globality. Secular temporality serves as a vehicle for the ideology of the secular state or the civil society, while religious temporality serves as a vehicle for the religious beliefs and practices of the population. Duara uses the phrase "redemptive transnationalism"[21] to refer to the latter, the temporality of those adhering to the religion of the homeland, who are seen as keepers and propagators of this faith.

The way the temporality of the center relates to the temporality of the periphery depends on the historical conditions on the ground. Where mosque life is already established, individual piety finds an infrastructure, and the presence of clergy or congregation helps sustain attendance. The degree of adherence to homeland time reflects the weakness, strength, and content of the connections. Sometimes the content, but not the form of the connection is accepted, which becomes a matter of interpretation, if not a matter of adaptation or modernization.

Because the logic of globalization applies to a much larger domain and aims at multiple goals, it may come into conflict with the logic of a local site that is geared toward a specific population. Local time brings its own contingency, despite it being a node in a global flow. Global time expresses itself through local time, which serves as its infrastructure, but which also gives it its local cadence. Mishra addresses one aspect of this contention between the local and the global in the realm of social policy. He argues that "social policy emerges as a major issue of contention between global capitalism and the democratic nation state."[22]

The chronopolis is not the only unit that must congeal to the globality of its temporality. The dominant civil week and its Christian attendant are part of global flows, as well. The civil week is global through its multiple connections with the rest of the world for political relations, commercial transactions, and social interaction, while the Christian week reflects the global or universal spread of the faith. In this sense, too, the global chronopolis is shaped by its entrenchment in a local site and by the relations it maintains with other globalized local units. Therefore, temporal policies that are geared toward the recognition and validation of compatible asynchronicity are more likely to bring harmonious coexistence than those that seek assimilation and conformity.

Time equity

In this book, I have attempted to show the labyrinthine contours, corridors, and parameters of the chronopolis, its relations with both the mainstream and the homeland, and how its temporality is shaped by both. I have also demonstrated how ethnic time is reshaping the face of the Western metropolis, and how the different calendars, Gregorian and ethnic, are naturalizing our perceptions of time and the rhythm of our everyday life. In the broadest sense, the issue underlying the relations between hegemonic and subaltern diasporic temporalities that we have been examining, between the metropolis and its varied chronopolises, is the issue of time equity. Time equity has emerged as an ethnic project undertaken to undermine time subjugation that is a factor of discrimination and to bring about the advent of a temporally multiculturalized and multiculturally temporized democracy.

Time discrimination has always been a factor that sustains the architecture of Western democracy. Time discrimination presupposes the existence of different time-reckoning systems that coexist within the same social milieu, the hierarchy of time systems that elevates one and necessarily downgrades the others, and the hegemony of one over the subalternization of the others. These time systems are therefore accorded different values in society, and through them, individuals are placed in a hierarchy of unequal status positions. Time inequity reflects the subaltern position of minoritzed groups and undermines their ability to compete fairly with those in the mainstream system, who are placed in an advantageous temporal position. This enhances the inherent inequality that is built in the social system in respect to temporal practices. Equality of access, not of conditions, heralded by the principle of participatory and consti- tutional democracy, cannot be achieved in such a social system.

This temporal inequity takes various shapes in society and has a negative effect on those so confined. It is often a cover-up for exploitation. Such is often the case of women who are involved in the same line of work as men, but are not paid the same salary. This form of exploitation values the time of some while devaluing that of others. It creates a hierarchy, distributes people in various unequal positions, and places some individuals in a time lag *vis-à-vis* others. Time is slowed down to decelerate the pace of promotions of some, or is accelerated to hasten the pace of promotions for others.

Time inequity perverts the trajectory of the diasporic community because it assigns it to an inferior position where it cannot compete fairly with the mainstream community and where it is forced to expe- rience a time lag *vis-à-vis* the hegemonic community. Since commu- nity time is a function of the continuity of cultural traditions of the homeland, the majority deglobalizes them and relocalizes them so that it can justify its practices and discriminate against those groups with a different time-reckoning system for the purpose of main- taining its hegemony. This problem of temporal inequity, justified according to the rules of a local context, is a general phenomenon that manifests itself with its distinctive features in different local sites. This problem appears with its local coloration in such sites as Jerusalem, Paris, Beijing, Tokyo, Tehran, Cairo, Manila, Bombay, Lagos, Rabat, Istanbul, Buenos Aires, and, of course, New York.

While the theorization of the problem helps us to understand its spatial parameters, practical ways of dealing with it do not come about too easily. In this pursuit, Glennie and Thrift have called for "empirical research into the interfaces among various timing traditions in societies that employ time keeping to varying degrees in varying contexts."[23] They further propose the need "to examine the specificity and range of power relations which constitute (and are constituted by) practices about time," as well as "various subcultures with different temporal discourses and different means of employing and interpreting them in different contexts; and the uneven meeting of these subcultures in particular places and contexts of power."[24] They argue that time must be seen as a "kind of technology for ordering and disciplining society," and they conclude that we are moving away "from, rather towards, the hiatus of a synchronized modernity."[25]

While one recognizes these temporal differences between diverse groups, that recognition should not lead one to identify community with homogeneity. Ethnic communities are not temporally homogeneous. This is why a chronopolis does not necessarily include all the individuals of the same ethnicity or ancestry who live in the city, but may also include individuals of other ancestry. Greenhouse warns us as to where such a pitfall may lead. She notes that "dividing 'community' from 'diversity' on these tacit racial grounds creates space for both the normal, negative meanings of diversity (as disorderly) and their transformed positive meanings as the canvas of the state's agency."[26] The recognition of diversity within the diasporic community complicates the mathematics of social relations and the problematization of time equity as a democratic project.

The plurality of temporalities in society is now interpreted through a reproblematization of the practice of citizenship. Citizenship is the angle through which asymmetric temporalities can best be understood. In this light, Shapiro speaks of "political interaction as a continuous negotiation of co-presence among those with diverse ways of being-in-time" and defines the nation "as a set of disjunctive temporal performances."[27] In such a context, the role of the state involves – among other things – "managing disjoint temporalities."[28] As a result of this, the urban community "cannot exist in one coherent temporal trajectory."[29]

No matter how messy the infrastructure of social relations is, the time issue cannot be put aside, because it is at the center of the reconstitution of the democratic project as the Rest meets the West in the West. As Adam reminds us, "temporal equity, temporal rights, negotiations over temporal conflicts and their arbitration would be integral to a temporized democracy."[30] The shift here is not to identify time equity as an ethnic problem, but rather as democracy's problem. This issue is intrinsic to a multicultural practice of democracy, and not simply a peripheral problem that concerns and affects only a handful of individuals. Until the issue of equity is resolved, the democratic process will remain an unfinished project of modernity.

Notes

Chapter 1

1. See for example, Massey and Denton (1993); Wilson (1987); Logan and Molotch (1987); and Laguerre (1999).

2. Bergmann (1992, p. 126) notes that there is "a lack of investigations of the temporal structures of social subsystems and subcultures that could support analyses of entire societies from the viewpoint of the sociology of time."

3. See for example, Lewis (1888); and Raucher (1994).

4. Abu-Lughod (1989); and Wallerstein (1974).

5. See Kern (1983, pp. 89–92) and Nguyen (1992, p. 30).

6. Richards (1998); Colson (1926); Parisot and Suagher (1996); and Maiello (1996).

7. Panth notes that "Gregory, by his Papal Bull Inter Gravissimas, of February 24, 1582, decreed that the day following Thursday, October 4, 1582, would be called Friday, October 15, 1582" Panth (1944, p. 71).

8. I am referring here to the ordinances that forbid people from engaging in certain tasks on Sunday; see on this issue, Laband and Heinbuch (1987).

9. One may develop a new typology of diasporas based on the time factor: diasporas whose civil and religious calendars are not in harmony with the Gregorian calendar because they follow the lunar or lunisolar motions (Israelis and Saudi Arabians, for example) while the Western calendar follows the solar motions; diasporas whose civil calendar is the same as the Western calendar and whose religious calendar is different (Russian immigrants); diasporas whose religious calendar is the same as the Gregorian calendar and whose civil calendar is different (Christians from Muslim states who have emigrated to the United States); diasporas who in their homeland use a double calendar, Western and non-Western (Chinese immigrants); diasporas whose weekly rest day corresponds to that of the Western calendar (Turkish immigrants) and whose weekly rest day does not correspond to that of the Western calendar (Jewish immigrants);

diasporas for whom the structure of the week does not constitute a problem because no weekly worship day is designated in their native calendar (Vietnamese immigrants); and diasporas for whom the structure of the Western civil week constitutes a problem (Iranian immigrants). From the perspective of time, some diasporas are better off than others in terms of their adaptation in American society. Those diasporas that have a civil calendar similar to the Western calendar do not have to deal with this asynchronicity problem. So one may develop a different typology from this temporal angle: those for whom the week cannot be renegotiated because of religious obligations; those for whom one month of the year brings much hardship in relations to their work schedule because of the obligation to fast during Ramadan; and those for whom the entire year harbors difficulties because of subalternized religious duties and secular festivals that are located all along and in the interstices of the Gregorian calendar. For alternative typologies of diasporas, see Medam (1993); Marientras (1985, pp. 215–26); and Safran (1991).

10. On globality, see Featherstone (1990); Robertson (1992); and Albrow (1996).
11. Zerubavel (1981, 1985).
12. Bhabha (1990, p. 302).
13. Hassard (1990, p. xiii).
14. Mercure (1995, p. 25). The use of a double calendar in the community with mainstream and ethnic dates does not necessarily ease the difficulty. Such a practice sometimes brings more confusion than clarity in the transactional deployment of everyday life. A Chinese American student once told me that he went to pick up his girlfriend for a party they were invited to and learned embarrassingly that they came to the host's house at the wrong time. The date of the party was selected on the basis of the Chinese calendar, and not the Western one. Since that incident, when he is invited by a Chinese person, he always inquires which calendar he or she is using.
15. Bhabha (1990, p. 303).
16. Guha (1998, p. 158).
17. For recent reviews of the literature on the sociology of Time, see Nowotny, (1992); Sue (1994); and Pronovost (1996).
18. Bhabha (1990, p. 303).

19. Hassard (1990, p. xi).
20. Gurvitch (1990, p. 40). See also, Durkheim (1965).
21. Sorokin and Merton (1990, p. 66).
22. Hassard (1990, p. x).
23. Halbwachs (1992, p. 104).
24. Fabian (1983, pp. 30–1); and Mercure (1995, p. 24).
25. Lewis and Weigart (1990, p. 83).
26. Coser and Coser (1990, p. 191).
27. Rutz (1992).
28. See Foucault (1977).
29. Parry (1940).
30. Wilson (1988). Zerubavel (1985, pp. 28–35).
31. Zeitlin (1930).
32. The matter becomes somewhat blurred if we were to introduce the notion of cybertime into the discussion. See Douglis *et al.* (1998); Corcoran (1996). What would a cyberday, cybermonth, or cyberyear mean? Until recently, we have made a clear distinction between daylight time and night time by investing daytime with labor or public activities and by considering nighttime as private or free time, except for those who work in different shifts. A day with a continuous twenty-four hours in cybertime does not have to start at midnight and does not have to end at midnight, since one can arrange one's time in any way one wishes to do so. In the virtual arena of the information superhighway, "Web weeks" follow a cycle different from the civil week. Lee and Liebnau (2000).
33. Padilla (1997); Culp (1994). For a discussion on border crossing in the context of "coloniality," see Mignolo (2000).
34. See for example, Elias (1992); Giddens (1991); Thompson (1967); and Rifkin (1987).
35. For some thoughtful discussions on the modernity issue, see Featherstone *et al.* (1995).
36. Levinas (1987); Gell (1993).
37. On the concept of mixed times, see Pieterse (1995, p. 51); Calderon (1988, pp. 225–9).
38. Laguerre (2000).
39. Modelski (1994, p. 248).
40. Laidi (1997, p. 11).
41. Virilio (1997, p. 286).

42. *Ibid.*
43. Giddens (1990).
44. *Ibid.*, p. 21.
45. Harvey (1989).
46. See for example, Zerubavel (1982).
47. Luhmann (1982. pp. 289–324).
48. Adam (1996, pp. 322–3).
49. Castells (1996).
50. *Ibid.*, p. 434.
51. *Ibid.*, p. 464.
52. Basch *et al.* (1994); Vertovec (1999).
53. Cox (1997).
54. On the global city concept, see Sassen (1991); Knox Taylor (1995); Eade (1997).
55. For a definition of the "ethnopolis" and a discussion of their integration in American society, see Laguerre (2000).
56. Rudolf and Piscatori (1997).

Chapter 2

1. Haas (1992).
2. Hinman (1838). See also, Laband and Heinbuch (1987, p. 8).
3. Trumbull (1876).
4. Strand (1979).
5. Bauckham (1982, pp. 312–41).
6. Beckwith and Stott (1978).
7. Stiles notes that "it was not until 321 AD that the week became officially recognized when Constantine the Great . . . sanctioned the pagan 'Dies Solis' as the Christian day of rest" (Stiles, 1933, p. 30).
8. Bacchiocchi (1977, p. 183).
9. Porter notes that "for generations to come, there would still be isolated communities of Jewish Christians who would not only observe the Lord's Day, but also the Sabbath" (Porter, 1960, p. 18).
10. Bacchiocchi (1977, p. 309).
11. Riesenfeld (1959, pp. 210–18 and 1970, pp. 111–37).
12. Zerubavel (1985).
13. See the Confession of Augsburg (Luther, 1530).
14. Bacchiocchi (1977, pp. 165–212).

15. Danielou (1948) and Congar (1948, pp. 131–80). There are three major contentions over the orthodoxy and orthopraxis of the Christian Sunday. The first questions the authority of the church to shift the Sabbath from the last day of the week (Saturday) to the first day (Sunday). Some Christian denominations such as the Seventh Day Adventists contest this change by arguing that it has no biblical basis. Bacchiocchi (1977).

The second contention questions the time during which the early Christians met for their common corporate worship. It was on the first day of the week and in the evening. See Bauchkam (1982b, pp. 221–50). The problem that arises here is with the definition of a day. For Beckwith and Stott (1978, p. 84), "it is impossible to be certain how long the early Christians continued the Jewish attitude of treating the day as beginning at dusk or whether they soon abandoned that for the Roman system." If we use the Jewish definition of a day, and the majority of the early Christians were Jews, we arrive with the conclusion that the primitive church met on Saturday evening. If we follow the Roman or Western definition of the day, they would have met on Sunday evening (1965).

The third contention revolves around the definition of "rest" on Sunday. It is here that civil Sunday provides the legal context for the practice of rest on Sunday and where the boundaries between the two are blurred. Clearly, the Jewish definition and practice of rest on the Sabbath day is stricter than the definition adopted by the Christians. Christians, in their practice of Sunday rest, tend to follow the ebb and flow of modern life and the restrictions imposed on society by the blue laws.

16. Rordorf (1968).
17. Huber (1958). See also, Rordorf, (1968, p. 167).
18. Ward (1960, p. 85).
19. Porter (1960, p. 25).
20. On the conversion from the Julian to the Gregorian calendar in the American colonies, see Franklin (1752/1753).
21. For typologies of diasporas, see Cohen (1997) and Safran (1991).
22. Laguerre (1999).
23. Hanchard (1999).
24. The general definition of the civil day is that of the artificial day or clock day. That is, the duration of time that goes from

midnight to midnight. This definition, although the most common, is not, however, always held up in matters of labor and insurance contracts, for example. In construction law, "a calendar day includes the time from midnight to midnight" (p. 12). In labor law, "a week means seven consecutive days beginning with Monday" (art. 18 p. 56), while in construction law, "a week is the period of time between midnight Saturday and midnight of the following Saturday" (p. 17). In construction law, "working days as ordinarily used means the days as they succeed each other, exclusive of Sundays and holidays" (p. 13). The labor law also speaks of a "calendar week" or "payroll week" in matters of unemployment insurance.

25. A major difference between the Christian calendrical units and the civil calendrical units is provided by canon law. See Dube (1941) and Finnegan (1965). Canon law, which regulates the religious life of the Catholic faithful, provides its own definition of the day, week, month, and year. Canon 202 # 1 states: "in law, a day is understood to be a space of twenty-four hours, to be reckoned continuously and, unless expressly provided otherwise, it begins at midnight; a week is a space of seven days; a month is a space of thirty days, and a year a space of three hundred and sixty-five days, unless it is stated that the month and the year are to be taken as in the [Gregorian or Western] calendar" Sheehy (1995).

The canon law does recognize that its definition of the month and year, does not totally coincide with those of the civil calendar. The Catholic Church uses its own calendar to define these basic units of time, and also uses the civil calendar in reference to the shorter or longer months of the year as well as the leap years.

26. Stiles (1933).
27. Friedenberg ([1908], 1986).
28. For a brief history of the Muslim community in New York City, see Ferris (1995, pp. 793–5).
29. Sabbath, in *McKinney's Consolidated Laws of New York. Annotated. Book 19. General Business Law # 1 to 351* (1988, pp. 5–30).
30. Laband and Heinbuch (1987, p. 108).
31. Sabbath, in *McKinney's Consolidated Laws of New York* (1988, p. 12).

32. Blakely (1911, p. 112).
33. Laband and Heinbuch (1987, p. 113).
34. Sabbath, in *McKinney's Consolidated Laws of New York* (1988, p. 26).
35. *McKinney's Consolidated Laws of New York* (1999, p. 21).
36. *Ibid.*, p. 23.
37. Blakely (1911, p. 615).
38. Friedenberg ([1908], 1986, p. 1).
39. *Ibid.*, p. 16.
40. *Ibid.*, p. 9.
41. *Ibid.*, pp. 10 and 15.
42. *Ibid.*, pp. 14 and 18.
43. For a comprehensive examination of the legal parameters of the blue laws, see Ringgold (1891).
44. Theologically, however, even these boundaries are far from settled. What is deemed permissible as work on Sunday and not permissible: emergency versus routine work, or continuous work dictated by industry that cannot be stopped, like attending to an electric plant or serving as a nurse in a hospital?
45. For a discussion of this issue among Catholic theologians, see Kiesling (1970).
46. The lobbying movement for either the maintenance or repeal of the blue laws has attracted individuals and groups who saw potential advantages or disadvantages that may contribute to or impede their religious, social, political, or economic pursuits. See Barron (1965) and Laband and Heinbuch (1987).

    While the Christian majority has fought for the maintenance of the blue laws because the legal day of rest facilitates the practice of the day of worship that they observe, some non-Christian groups (and Christian Sabbatarians) have lobbied to prevent the application of such Sunday legislation to their communities. So the struggle of these dissidents has not been for the elimination of the blue laws, but for their confinement to the activities and practices of the majority group. With such an arrangement, opponents have sought to continue to hold their day of worship or prayer on Friday or Saturday, as the case might be, while using Sunday as a regular day of work.

    Various factors, however, have militated against the maintenance of the blue laws and, in the process, have opposed the interests of small retailers to those of large businesses. As a matter of fact, the existence of the blue laws has caused different reactions from among the mercantile class. Owners of large businesses, by and large, have been in favor of the repeal of such laws in order to attract the Sunday clientele to their operations, while small businesses (many owned by religious or ethnic minorities) have fought for the maintenance of the blue laws in order to protect their market niches. See Kay and Morris (1987); Barnes (1984); Barnes and Chopoorian (1987); McNiel and Yu (1989). These small retailers believe that the blue laws, by allowing people with a different Sabbath day to operate their stores on Sunday, make it possible for them to carve a protected niche whereby they can make a profit without having to compete at least one day per week with the large stores. Other owners of small stores have opted for the maintenance of the blue laws for staffing reasons, afraid that they might be forced to work seven days a week. While it is easy for a large department store to spread its workforce across seven days, it is more costly for 'mom-and-pop' shops to do so because the same members of the family would have to add Sunday as a day of work to their schedule or else they must hire extra labor that would eat up part of their meager profits. See Solis (1985, p. 25). These different positions have come about not only because of the projection of profit maximization, but also because of the strategies by small retailers to minimize operating costs. With such an arrangement, weekly revenues are preserved, but distributed over a smaller number of days. See Tullock (1975) and Moorehouse (1984).

Focusing on either religious groups or small and large businesses, as we have done so far, is not sufficient to understand the multiple causes that explain the elimination or repeal of the blue laws in some communities. For Price and Yandle (1987, pp. 407–14), "changes in the labor markets, particularly that relate to unions and to women workers, are fundamental to the repeal of the laws." They argue that the participation of women in the labor force "increased the demand for Sunday shopping" and for "expanded shopping hours." On the supply side, they identified the establishment of chain stores in small towns as an added incentive for Sunday shopping. They conclude that retailers, Christian groups, organizations associated with the tourist industry, female workers, and one-party-dominated legislative bodies are the combined variables that played a decisive role in the repeal of blue laws in various states of the Union.

47. To have a glimpse of the way in which the Court has dealt with this issue see the following: Stadtmauer (1994); Raucher (1994); Kushner (1981); Gregory (1981); Redman (1991); and Johns (1967).

48. For the Catholic Church's positions on the blue laws, see Drinan (1959, p. 411; 1960, pp. 629–30; 1961, p. 505; and 1963, p. 210).

49. Strum (1992).

50. *The New York Times* (1997).

51. *Ibid.*, (1993).

52. *Ibid.*, (1995).

53. Caher (1999).

54. Lynwander (1991).

55. *The New York Times* (1994).

56. Rudolph (1997, pp. 1–24).

57. John Paul II (1998).

58. Cullman (1964, p. 62).

59. Robertson (1992, p. 100).

Chapter 3

1. Frommer and Frommer (1995, p. 178).

2. Beckwith and Stott (1978).

3. Walter A. Lurie, *Strategies for Survival: Principles of Jewish Community Relations.* New York: KTAV Publishing House Inc., 1982, p. 62.

4. Cohen (1992, p. 216).

5. Glazer (1957, p. 118).

6. Yaffe (1968, p. 119).

7. Blau (1976, p. 108).

8. Sorin (1992).

9. Stiles (1933, p. 131).

10. Sarna and Dalin (1997, p. 139).

11. In this light, one might add that in the evolution of the two day week-end Jews have had a long experience with such a condition before it begins to be a secular practice of the state. One can then speak of the unattended consequences of the blue laws. While their aim was to police Sunday as a mandatory day of rest, they

contributed to the shaping of a double day of rest back to back
which provides the structure of the weekend.

12. Sorin (1992, p. 74).
13. Stiles (1933, p. 132).
14. Cohen (1992, p. 215).
15. Gay (1965, p. 66).
16. Sorin (1992, p. 182).
17. Stiles (1933, p. 132).
18. Yaffe (1968, p. 102).
19. Bourne (1987) and Bondi (1993, pp. 84–101).
20. Barth had earlier emphasized the notion of boundary mainte-
    nance as the angle through which we can decipher the produc-
    tion of ethnic identity.
21. Sarna and Dalin (1997, p. 214).
22. As the Synagogue Council of America, in an *amicus curiae* brief
    filed in 1961 with the Supreme Court of the United States, ex-
    plained, non-Christian students confront a dilemma in matters
    related to prayers and religious instructions in public schools.
    It argues that the school has become a site where battles for the
    supremacy of one religion over the others are fought: Religious
    education is not neutral on the temporal issue. The instructors
    teach the students about the importance of the Sunday as the
    peak day of the Christian week. According to the brief, those who
    do not belong to that faith are likely to feel subalternized. The
    issue is that non-Christian students share the secular time of the
    state by participating in the institutional services of the secular
    state without sharing the religious time of the state when the
    latter is identified with a specific religion. The solution proposed
    for the dilemma is to provide the students with release time.
    Release time means allowing them to remain in the shared
    secular time of the state, but allowing them to attend to their
    own religious time. This process is not the same as dismissed time
    whereby they could leave the school premises.
23. Cohen (1997).
24. Graham and Graham (1995).
25. Strand (1979).
26. Bacchiocchi (1977).
27. Sarna and Dalin (1997, p. 139).
28. Kaplan (1957, p. 106).

29. Olitzky (1985).
30. Markovitz (1969).
31. *Ibid.*, p. 142.
32. Mark 15:42, "Now when the evening had come, because it was the Preparation Day, that is, the day before the sabbath." John 19:14 and 42, "Now it was the Preparation Day of the Passover, and about the sixth hour." And "So there they laid Jesus, because of the Jews' Preparation Day, for the tomb was nearby."
33. Kliger (1992, p. 101).
34. Stiles (1933, p. 133).
35. Golden (1965, p. 10).
36. Sherman (1961, p. 162).
37. Powell (1995, p. 17).
38. A variation of temporal substitution, mechanical substitution occurs when a mechanical device that it is forbidden to use on the Sabbath is set so that one would not need to operate the forbidden object. This is the situation in some Jewish-owned hotels in Manhattan and in Israel, where the elevator is set to stop at every floor on Sabbath. A Jewish guest does not need to touch any button to get to his or her floor. I was also told that in some Jewish homes, the television may be set to turn itself on at a specific hour without any human manipulation to allow members to watch a football game or other forms of entertainment.
39. Golden (1965, p. 92).
40. Pieterse (1995).
41. Jacobs (1995, p. 148).
42. Joseph M. Smith, etc., *et al.* v. Community Board No. 14, *et al.* Supreme Court, Special Term, Queens County, Part 1. July 8, 1985. 491 New York Supplement 2d Series 58–1 (Sup. 1985).
43. American Civil Liberties Union of New Jersey and Deborah D. Jacoby, Plaintiffs v. City of Long Branch, *et al.*, Defendants. Congregation Brothers of Israel, Inc., Rabbi Tobias Roth, *et al.*, Defendant-Intervenors. United States District Court, District of New Jersey. Civil No 87–1822, September 22, 1987.
44. Wigoder (1989, p. 231).
45. The *eruv* thus brings a new dimension to our understanding of the genealogy of segregated ethnic space. To explain spatial segregation in reference to minoritized groups, the mainstream sociological approach (phenomenological, structuralist, or

Marxist) has been to blame the structure of domination that prevents homogenization or spatial integration as having been
imposed from above and to downplay cultural factors because
they are shaped within a context of structural constraints. The
eruv indicates some partial evidence that spatial segregation in a
few cases also has resulted from the internal religious logic of a
segment of the diasporic group. Here, ghettoized space may be
achieved to circumscribe rabbinical laws pertaining to the observance of the Sabbath and to engage in activities that otherwise
could be constructed as infractions to that religious legal regime.
Here, secular Jews ask the mainstream to intervene on their
behalf to prevent self-imposed Orthodox Jewish spatial ghettoization to the extent it might directly or indirectly affect them.

46. Boroff (2000, p. 34A).
47. Wigoder (1989, p. 231).
48. Ibid. (pp. 230–1) and Jacobs (1995, p. 148).
49. Joseph M. Smith, etc., *et al.* v. Community Board No. 14, *et al.*,
    op. cit., p. 585.
50. Affidavit of plaintiff Joseph M. Smith, dated March 9, 1985, cited
    in Joseph M. Smith, etc., *et al.* v. Community Board No. 14, *et al.*,
    p. 585.
51. Boroff (2000, p. 34A).
52. Castells (1997); Friedman (1994); and Hall (1997, pp. 41–68).
53. Meyer and Geschiere (1999, pp. 1–15).
54. The Central Conference of American Rabbis (1947, p. 31).
55. Biale (1999).

Chapter 4

1. This chapter is a revised version of a paper presented at the International Conference "Diasporas: Transnational Identity and the
   Politics of the Homeland" organized by the William Saroyan
   Chair in Armenian Studies and the Berkeley Program in Soviet
   and Post-Soviet Studies and held at the University of California
   at Berkeley, November 12–13, 1999. I am grateful to Hatem
   Bazian, Hamid Algar, Beshara Doumani, Ali H. Alyami and
   Stephan H. Astourian for their thoughtful contribution to this
   chapter.
2. It is not only in New York that Muslim places of worship are
   mushrooming (see Metcalf (1996, pp. 204–16)). A similar

phenomenon has been observed in the San Francisco Bay area as well. Hermansen (1994, p. 190) provides a profile of the Muslim organization in the San Francisco Bay Area: "The overall Muslim community in the San Francisco Bay area comprises over one hundred thousand persons with a total of perhaps fifteen functioning Islamic Centers or mosques including Masjid al-Islam (Oakland), Hussaini Center (San Jose), Masjid Muhammad (Oakland), Masjid An-Noor (Santa Clara), Masjid Jamea (San Francisco), Masjid Nur (Richmond), Islamic Center of San Jose, Hayward Masjid, Islamic Center of San Francisco, Islamic Center of Freemont, American Muslim Mission (San Francisco), Fiju Muslim Mosque (South San Francisco). Masjid Abi Bakr al-Siddiq (Berkeley), and two student groups at the University of California at Berkeley."

3. Smith (1999).
4. On the reasons given for the shift from Friday to Sunday as a day of rest in Muslim countries, see for Lebanon, Ziyadah (1996) and for Turkey, Rippin (1993, p. 131).
5. Zerubavel (1985, p. 4).
6. Ferris (1994, p. 220).
7. For a genealogy of the Friday prayer, see Goitein (1983, pp. 592–4; and 1958, pp. 488–500).
8. *The Holy Qur'an* edited by Maulana Muhammad Ali. Lahore, Pakistan: Ahmadiyyah Anjuman Isha'at Islam, 1991.
9. See on this, Ferris (1994, pp. 209–30); and Haddad and Lummis (1987).
10. Goitein (1966, p. 111).
11. Wensinck (1954).
12. Goddard (1995, p. 89).
13. Goitein (1966, p. 112).
14. Ibid., p. 120.
15. Richards (1998, p. 234).
16. Freeman-Grenville (1963, p. 3).
17. Canadian Muslims have also made use of Sunday for similar reasons. It is reported that "in some cities, a Sunday noon gathering is held that at least allows them an unofficial congregational prayer on the one day all Muslims are theoretically free to attend" (Hogben (1983, p. 113)).
18. Elkholy (1966).

19. Haddad (1983, p. 73); and Abraham *et al.* (1983, p. 173).
20. Haddad (1983, p. 76).
21. Abraham *et al.* (1983, p. 173).
22. Lahaj (1994, p. 309).
23. Abraham *et al.* (1983, p. 173).
24. Anway (1998, p. 188).
25. Not all Muslims see these obstacles as inconveniences in a negative light. Some prefer to see them as challenges that can draw one closer to Allah because of the extra effort that is needed to accomplish the prayers, see Metcalf (1996, pp. 1–27).
26. In her interview with French Muslims, Cesari was told a number of circumstances that may justify the jamming of the prayers (workplace constraints, menstrual period, postpartum period, to name a few). See Cesari (1997, p. 137); and Boyer (1998, p. 190).
27. For analyses of gendered time, see for example Davies (1990); Forman and Sowton (1989); Kristeva (1981); and Sullivan (1997).
28. For an elaboration of this argument, see Bloul (1996, pp. 234–50).
29. Rowbotham (1989, p. 148).
30. Young (1998).
31. Hermansen (1994, p. 180).
32. For some background materials on the framing of the gender issue among Muslim women, see Smith (1980).
33. Rippin (1993, p. 131).
34. Naff (1985).
35. Haddad and Lummis (1987, p. 19).
36. Ibid., p. 77.
37. Voll (1991, p. 207).
38. Husain and Vogelaar (1994, p. 246).
39. Abraham *et al.* (1983, p. 166).
40. Hermansen (1994, p. 178).
41. The Muslim population in Paris provides a point of comparison with the occurrences in New York. In Paris, the Muslim population has maintained a presence in the city for over a century. To reach the brethren both in the city or the nearby suburbs, the call to prayer is announced through Islamic radio programs choreographed by Muslim activists. Kepel speaks of the effort of the workplace to harmonize industrial time with Islamic time and explains how the Renault company has installed mosques

and prayer rooms in its factories and how the upper echelon of management has been sensitized to that issue to the extent that such a factor is integrated in their long-range planning and labor-relations policies. He also observes that similar policies were being implemented at Citroen and Simca, two other well known French firms. Kepel further notes that the institution of the Friday prayer has led to the transformation of the district where a popular mosque is located. He remarks that the Jean Pierre Timbaud Street becomes a very busy street on Friday. Many use the occasion to do their shopping in the Muslim stores, restaurants, bookshops, and meat shops. The area between the Couronne subway station and the location of the mosque is littered with Muslim commercial sites, and non-Muslim shops are being slowly pushed out to be replaced by Muslim stores Kepel (1987, pp. 9, 10, 150, 192). The establishment of a mosque in a neighborhood is a sure sign of the Arabization or Muslimization of the area.

42. Fischer and Abedi (1990, p. 311).
43. Richardson (1981).
44. Osman (1999, p. 4). In the San Francisco Bay Area, the Islamic calendar and prayer times calculations are distributed around the Iranian New Year (March 21) and in the other Muslim communities around the Ramadan period. The Islamic Calendar and Prayer Times are also published every Islamic year in *The Greater California American Muslims Fast Yellow Pages: Business Telephone Directory* (Mahmood 1998).
45. For background discussion on Islamic globalism, see Turner (1991).
46. Hermansen (1994, p. 194).
47. See, for example, Bencheikh (1998, p. 9).
48. Haddad (1983, p. 72).

Chapter 5

1. Gould (1997, p. 88).
2. Divali is a festival of lights celebrated by Trinidadian immigrants of East Indian origin in New York. On this Hindu festival, see Ericksen (1993).
3. Jacobs (1973, p. 8).
4. Simons (1985).

5. Moss (1995).
6. Rogers (1998).
7. Moss (1995).
8. Colloredo-Mansfeld (1998).
9. Guttierez and Fabre (1995).
10. Low (1996).
11. Ericksen (1993).
12. Bernasconi (1990); Rolland (2000).
13. Kula (1979).
14. Sarna (1998/9).
15. James (1997).
16. Guyotte and Posadas (1995).
17. Goddard (1995, p. 89).
18. Haddad (1983, p. 76).
19. *Ibid.*
20. See Bourdieu (1977).
21. Meijers (1987, p. 603).
22. Achelis (1955, p. 16).
23. Haddad and Lummis (1987, p. 91).
24. Chaichian (1997, p. 620).
25. Jacobs (1973, p. 91).
26. Pogrebin (1996, p. 135).
27. Sorin (1992, p. 77).
28. *Ibid.*, p. 174.
29. Bershtel and Graubard (1992, p. 101).
30. Blau (1976, p. 84).
31. Haddad and Lummis (1987, p. 77).
32. Schmemann (1998).
33. Moore (1975, pp. 143–4).
34. Berrol (1994, p. 54).
35. See Wiesenberg (1963, p. II); see also Brusca (1969, p. II).
36. Mitchell (1998).
37. Newman (1997, p. 140).
38. *Ibid.*, p. 122.
39. *Ibid.*, p. 131.
40. Held *et al.*, (1999).
41. James (1997).
42. Al-Qazzaz (1979, p. 49).
43. *Ibid.*

44. *Ibid.*, p. 41.
45. *Ibid.*, p. 40.
46. Appadurai (1996).
47. Castells (1989).
48. Featherstone (1990).
49. Beyer (1994); Tomlinson (1999, p. 40; and 1998).
50. See Robertson (1992; 1995).

Conclusion

1. Goldberg (1994); Willett (1998).
2. Taylor (1992).
3. Lewis (1888, p. 201).
4. "It is sufficient defense to a prosecution for work or labor on the first day of the week that the defendant uniformly keeps another day of the week as holy time, and does not labor on that day, and that the labor complained of was done in such manner as not to interrupt or disturb other persons in observing the first day of the week as holy time." Blakely (1911, p. 612).
5. Schissel (1999).
6. Goodstein (1999).
7. Newman (1999).
8. O'Harrow (1994).
9. *Wall Street Journal* (1996).
10. Shain (1999).
11. Held *et al.* (1999, p. 2).
12. Featherstone (1990, p. 10).
13. Robertson (1990, p. 19).
14. Castells (1989).
15. Appadurai (1996).
16. Badie (1995).
17. Meyer and Geschiere (1999, p. 14).
18. Held *et al.* (1999, pp. 20 and 331).
19. Kelly (1999, p. 268).
20. *Ibid.*, p. 259.
21. Duara (1999, p. 50).
22. Mishra (1999, p. 15).
23. Glennie and Thrift (1996).
24. *Ibid.*, p. 292.
25. *Ibid.*, p. 293.

26. Greenhouse (1996, p. 231).
27. Shapiro (2000).
28. *Ibid.*, p. 83.
29. *Ibid.*, p. 96.
30. Adam (1996).

References

Abraham, S. V., N. Abraham and B. Aswad (1983) The Southend: An Arab Muslim Working-Class Community. In S. Y. Abraham and N. Abraham (eds), *Arabs in the New World: Studies on Arab-American Communities*, Detroit: Wayne State University Press.

Abu-Lughod, J. (1989) *Before European Hegemony: The World System AD 1250–1350*. New York: Oxford University Press.

Achelis, E. (1955) *Of Time and the Calendar*. New York: Hermitage House.

Adam, B. (1990) *Time and Social Theory*. Cambridge: Polity Press.

Adam, B. (1992) Modern Times: The Technology Connection and its Implications for Social Theory. *Time and Society* 1(2), pp. 175–91.

Adam, B. (1994) Beyond Boundaries: Reconceptualizing Time in the Face of Global Challenges. *Social Science Information* 33(4), pp. 597–620.

Adam, B. (1996) Beyond the Present: Nature, Technology and the Democratic Ideal. *Time and Society* 5(3), pp. 319–38.

Adams, P. (1999) Bringing Globalization Home: A Homeowner in the Information Age. *Urban Geography* 20(4), pp. 356–76.

Albrow, M. (1996) *The Global Age*. Stanford: Stanford University Press.

Al-Qazzaz, A. (1979) *Transnational Links Between the Arab Community in the US and the Arab World*. Sacramento: Cal Central Press.

American Civil Liberties Union of New Jersey and Deborah D. Jacoby, Plaintiffs v. City of Long Branch, *et al.*, Defendants. Congregation Brothers of Israel, Inc., Rabbi Tobias Roth, *et al.*, Defendant-Intervenors. United States District Court, District of New Jersey. Civil No 87–1822, September 22, 1987.

Anway, C. L. (1998) American Women Choosing Islam. In Y. Y. Haddad and J. L. Esposito (eds), *Muslims on the Americanization Path*, Atlanta: Scholars Press.

Appadurai, A. (1996) *Modernity at Large: Cultural Dimensions of Globalization*. Minneapolis: University of Minnesota Press.

Baal-Schem, J. and D. Shinar (1998) The Telepresence Era: Global Village or "Media Slums"? *IEEE Technology and Society Magazine*, Spring 1998, pp. 28–35.

Bacchiocchi, S. (1977) *From Sabbath to Sunday: A Historical Investigation of the Rise of Sunday Observance in Early Christianity.* Rome: The Pontifical Gregorian University Press.

Badie, B. (1995) *La Fin des Territoires: Essai sur le Desordre International et sur l'Utilite Sociale du Respect.* Paris: Fayard.

Barley, S. R. (1988) On Technology, Time and Social Order: Technologically Induced Change in the Temporal Organization of Radiological Work. In F. A. Dubinskas (ed.), *Making Time: Ethnographies of High-Technology Organizations*, pp. 123–69. Philadelphia: Temple University Press.

Barnes, N. G. (1984) New Shopper Profiles: Implications of Sunday Sales. *Journal of Small Business Management* 22, pp. 32–9.

Barnes, N. G. and J. Chopoorian (1987) Small Retailers and Sunday Sales. *Journal of Small Business Management* 22, pp. 40–6.

Barron, J. A. (1965) Sunday In North America. *Harvard Law Review* 79 (November): pp. 42–54.

Basch, L. *et al.; Nations Unbound.* New York: Gordon and Breach, 1994.

Bauckham, R. J. (1982a) Sabbath and Sunday in the Protestant Tradition. In D. A. Carson (ed.), *From Sabbath to Lord's Day: A Biblical, Historical and Theological Investigation*, pp. 312–41. Grand Rapids: Zondervan Publishing House.

Bauchkam, R. J. (1982b) The Lord's Day. In D. A. Carson (ed.), *From Sabbath to Lord's Day*, pp. 221–50. Grand Rapids: Zondervan Publishing House.

Becker, G. (1965) A Theory of the Allocation of Time. *Economic Journal* 75, pp. 493–517.

Beckwith, R. T. and W. Stott (1978) *This is the Day. The Biblical Doctrine of the Christian Sunday in its Jewish and Early Church Setting.* London: Marshall, Morgan and Scott.

Bencheikh, S. (1998) *Marianne et le Prophete: L'Islam dans la France Laique.* Paris: Grasset.

Bergmann, W. (1992) The Problem of Time in Sociology: An Overview of the Literature on the State of Theory and Research on the Sociology of Time, 1900–82. *Time and Society* 1(1), pp. 81–134.

Bernasconi, A. (1990) Cofradias Religiosas e Identidad en la inmigracion Italiana en Argentina. *Estudios Migratorios Latinoamericanos* 5(14), pp. 211–24.

Berrol, S. (1994) *East Side/East End: Eastern European Jews in London and New York, 1870–1920.* Westport: Praeger.

Bershtel, S. and A. Graubard (1992) *Saving Remnants: Feeling Jewish in America.* New York: The Free Press.

Beyer, P. (1994) *Religion and Globalization.* London: Sage.

Bhabha, H. (1990) DissemiNation: Time, Narrative, and the Margins of the Modern Nation. In H. Bhabha (ed.), *Nation and Narration.* New York: Routledge.

Biale, D. (1999) Notes on the Jewish Millennium. *Tikkun* 14(6), pp. 60–1.

Blakely, W. A. (1911) *American State Papers Bearing on Sunday Legislation.* Washington DC: The Religious Liberty Association.

Blau, J. L. (1976) *Judaism in America: From Curiosity to Third Faith.* Chicago: University of Chicago Press.

Bloul, R. (1996) Engendering Muslim Identities: Deterritorialization and the Ethnicization Process in France. In B. Metcalf (ed.), *Making Muslim Space in North America and Europe.* Berkeley: University of California Press.

Bollier, D. (ed.) (1997) *The Networked Society: How Technologies are Transforming Markets, Organizations, and Social Relationships.* Washington DC: The Aspen Institute.

Bondi, L. (1993) Locating Identity Politics. In M. Keith and S. Pile (eds), *Place and the Politics of Identity.* New York: Routledge, pp. 84–101.

Boroff, L. (2000) Sparks Still Fly as Palo Alto Mulls Decision on Eruv. *Jewish Bulletin*, February 18.

Borst, A. (1993) *The Ordering of Time.* Chicago: University of Chicago Press.

Bourdieu, P. (1977) *Outline of a Theory of Practice.* Cambridge: Cambridge University Press.

Bourne, J. (1987) Homelands of the Mind: Jewish Feminism and Identity Politics. *Race and Class* 29, pp. 1–24.

Boyer, A. (1998) *L'Islam en France.* Paris: Presses Universitaires de France.

Brusca, A. J. (ed.) (1969) *Official Directory of the Board of Education of the City of New York 1968–1969.* New York: Board of Education.

Caher, J. (1999) Sunday Morning Beer Sales Get Push. *The Times Union*, January 30.

Calderon, F. (1988) America Latina, Identidad y Tiempos Mixtos, o como pensar la modernidad sin dejar de ser boliviano. In *Imagenes Desconocidas*. Buenos Aires: Ed CLACSO, pp. 225–9.

Carroll, L. P. (1998) What Sunday is it Anyway? *National Jesuit News*, November, pp. 8–9.

Castells, M. (1989) *The Informational City*. Oxford: Blackwell.

Castells, M. (1996) *The Rise of the Network Society*. Oxford: Blackwell.

Castells, M. (1997) *The Power of Identity*. Oxford: Blackwell.

Central Conference of American Rabbis (1947) *The Union Prayerbook for Jewish Worship*. Cincinnati: The Central Conference of American Rabbis.

Cesari, J. (1997) *Etre Musulman En France Aujourd'hui*. Paris: Hachette.

Chaichian, M. A. (1997) First Generation Iranian Immigrants and the Question of Cultural Identity: The Case of Iowa. *International Migration Review* 31(3), pp. 612–27.

Chidley, J. (1996) Cyber Time: Living by the Credo "Boot up, log on and connect," University Students are mounting a techno-revolution. *Maclean's* 109(48) (Nov. 25), pp. 68–9.

Clark, G. (1996) Managing your Retail Business in Internet Time. *Chain Store Age* 72(10), p. 112.

Cohen, J. B. (1996) Time, Space, Form and the Internet. *Editor and Publisher* 129(19), pp. 28–9.

Cohen, N. W. (1992) *Jews in Christian America: The Pursuit of Religious Equality*. New York: Oxford University Press.

Cohen, R. (1997) *Global Diasporas*. Seattle: University of Washington Press.

Colloredo-Mansfeld, R. (1998) The Handicraft Archipelago: Consumption, Migration, and the Social Organization of a Transnational Andean Ethnic Group. *Research in Economic Anthropology* 19, pp. 31–67.

Colson, F. H. (1926) *The Week*. Cambridge: Cambridge University Press.

Congar, Y. (1948) La Theologie du Dimanche, In *Le Jour du Seigneur*. Paris.

Corcoran, M. (1996) Digital Transformations of Time: The Aesthetics of the Internet. *Leonardo* 29(5), p. 375.

Coser, L. and R. Coser (1990) Time Perspective and Social Structure. In J. Hassard (ed.), *The Sociology of Time*. New York: St Martin's Press now Palgrave Macmillan.

Cox, K. R. (ed.) (1997) *Spaces of Globalization: Reasserting the Power of the Local*. New York: The Guilford Press.

Cullman, O. (1964) *Christ and Time: The Primitive Conception of Time and History*. Philadelphia: Westminster Press.

Culp, J. M. (1994) Colorblind Remedies and the Intersectionality of Oppression: Policy Arguments Masquerading as Moral Claims. *New York Law Review* 69(1), pp. 162–96.

Cusumano, M. A. and D. B. Yoffie (1998) *Competing on Internet Time: Lessons from Netscape and its Battle with Microsoft*. New York: The Free Press.

Cwerner, S. B. (2001) The Times of Migration. *Journal of Ethnic and Migration Studies* 27(1), pp. 7–36.

Danielou, J. (1948) La Typologie Millenariste de la Semaine dans le Christianisme Primitif. *Vigiliae Christianae* 2, pp. 1–16.

Davies, K. (1990) *Women and Time: The Weaving of the Strands of Everyday Life*. Aldershot: Avebury.

Dube, A. J. (1941) *The General Principles for the Reckoning of Time in Canon Law*. Washington DC: Catholic University to America Press.

Douglis, F., S. Chapin and J. Isaak (1998) Internet Research on Internet Time. *Computer* 31(11), pp. 76–8.

Drinan, R. (1959) Sunday Law in Jeopardy. *America* 101(6 June), p. 411.

Drinan, R. (1960) Sunday Laws and the First Amendment. *America* 104(19 August), pp. 629–30.

Drinan, R. (1961) The Court Judges Sunday Laws. *America* 105(21 Jan.), p. 505.

Drinan, R. (1963) *Religion, the Courts, and Public Policy*. New York: McGraw-Hill.

Duara, P. (1999) Transnationalism in the Era of Nation-States: China, 1900–1945. In B. Meyer and P. Geschiere (eds), *Globalization and Identity*. Oxford: Blackwell, p. 50.

Durkheim, E. (1965) *The Elementary Forms of Religious Life*. New York: Free Press.

Eade, J. (ed.) (1997) *Living the Global City: Globalization as a Local Process*. London: Routledge.

Elchardus, M. (1994) In Praise of Rigidity: On Temporal and Cultural Flexibility. *Social Science Information* 333(3), pp. 459–77.

Elias, N. (1992) *Time: An Essay*. Oxford: Blackwell.

Elkholy, A. A. (1966) *The Arab Moslems in the United States: Religion and Assimilation.* New Haven: College and University Press.

Ericksen, T. H. (1993) Formal and Informal Nationalism. *Ethnic and Racial Studies* 16(1), pp. 1–25.

Fabian, J. (1983) *Time and the Other: How Anthropology Makes its Object.* New York: Columbia University Press.

Failla, A. and S. Bagnara (1992) Information Technology, Decision-Time. *Social Science Information* 31(4), pp. 669–81.

Featherstone, M. (ed.) (1990) *Global Culture: Nationalism. Globalization and Modernity.* London: Sage.

Featherstone, M., S. Lash and R. Robertson (eds) (1995) *Global Modernities.* London: Sage.

Ferris, M. (1994) To Achieve the Pleasure of Allah: Immigrant Muslims in New York City, 1893–1991. In Y. Y. Haddad and J. Idleman (eds), *Muslim Communities in North America.* Albany: State University of New York Press.

Ferris, M. (1995) Muslims. In K. T. Jackson (ed.), *The Encyclopedia of New York City.* New Haven: Yale University Press, pp. 793–5.

Finnegan, J. T. (1965) *Selected Questions on the Computation of Time in Canon Law.* Rome: Officium Libri Catholici.

Fischer, M. M. J. and M. Abedi (1990) *Cultural Dialogues in Postmodernity and Tradition.* Madison: The University of Wisconsin Press.

Flannery, A. (ed.) (1992) *Vatican Council II.* Collegeville: The Liturgical Press.

Forman, F. J. and C. Sowton (eds) (1989) *Taking Our Time: Feminist Perspectives on Temporality.* Oxford: Pergamon Press.

Foucault, M. (1977) *Discipline and Punish: The Birth of the Prison.* New York: Random House.

Franklin, B. (1752/1753) *Poor Richard's Almanack.*

Freeman-Grenville, G. S. P. (1963) *The Muslim and Christian Calendars.* Oxford: Oxford University Press.

Friedenberg, A. M. ([1908], 1986) *The Sunday Laws of the United States and Leading Judicial Decisions Having Special Reference to the Jews.* Philadelphia: The Jewish Publication Society of America.

Friedman, J. (1994) *Cultural Identity and Global Process.* London: Sage.

Frommer, M. K. and H. Frommer. (1995) *Growing Up Jewish in America: An Oral History.* New York: Harcourt Brace and Company.

Gay, R. (1965) *Jews in America: A Short History.* New York: Basic Books.

Gell, A. (1993) *The Anthropology of Time.* Oxford: Berg.

Giddens, A. (1990) *The Consequences of Modernity.* Cambridge: Polity Press.

Giddens, A. (1991) *Modernity and Self-Identity.* Cambridge: Polity.

Glazer, N. (1957) *American Judaism.* Chicago: University of Chicago Press.

Glennie, P. and N. Thrift (1996) Reworking E. P. Thompson's "Time, Work-Discipline and Industrial Capitalism". *Time and Society* 5(3), pp. 275–99.

Goddard, H. (1995) *Christians and Muslims: From Double Standards to Mutual Understanding.* Surrey: Curzon Press.

Goitein, S. D. (1958) Le Culte du Vendredi Musulman: Son Arriere-Plan Social et Economique. *Annales, Economies, Societes, Civilisations,* pp. 488–500.

Goitein, S. D. (1966) The Origin and Nature of the Muslim Friday Worship. In *Studies in Islamic History and Institutions.* Leiden: E. J. Brill.

Goitein, S. D. (1983) "Djum'a", In B. Lewis, Ch. Pellat and J. Schacht (eds), *The Encyclopedia of Islam.* Leiden: E. J. Brill, vol II, pp. 592–4.

Goldberg, A. (1998) A Stitch in Time: Internet Years are Dead. *MC Technology Marketing Intelligence* 18(7), p. 16.

Goldberg, D. T. (1994) *Multiculturalism: A Critical Reader.* Oxford: Blackwell.

Golden, H. (ed.) (1965) *The Spirit of the Ghetto: Studies of the Jewish Quarter of New York by Hutchins Hapgood.* New York: Schocken Books.

Goodstein, L. (1999) ACLU Sues a School District for Closing on the Jewish High Holy Days. *The New York Times.* September 9, section A, page 20, column 1.

Gould, S. J. (1997) *Questioning the Millennium.* New York: Harmony Books.

Graham, P. C. and A. Graham (1995) Community Types, Community Typologies and Community Time. *Time and Society* 4(2), pp. 147–66.

Graham, S. and S. Marvin (1996) *Telecommunications and the City: Electronic Spaces, Urban Places.* New York: Routledge.

Graziano, C. (1999) There is No Time like Web time. *Informationweek* 766(December 20–27), p. 102.

Greenhouse, C. J. (1996) *A Moment's Notice: Time Politics Across Cultures*. Ithaca: Cornell University Press.

Gregory, D. L. (1981) The First Amendment Religious Clauses and Labor and Employment Law in the Supreme Court, 184 Term. *New York Law School Law Review* 31(1), pp. 1–36.

Guha, R. (1998) The Migrant's Time. *Postcolonial Studies* 1(2), pp. 155–60.

Gurvitch, G. (1990) The Problem of Time. In J. Hassard (ed.), *The Sociology of Time*. New York: St Martin's Press, now Palgrave.

Gurvitch, Georges (1961) *La Multiplicite des Temps Sociaux*. Paris: Centre de Documentation Universitaire.

Guttierez, R. A. and G. Fabre (eds) (1995) *Feasts and Celebrations in North American Ethnic Communities*. Albuquerque: University of New Mexico Press.

Guyotte, R. L. and B. M. Posadas (1995) Celebrating Rizal Day: The Emergence of a Filipino Tradition in Twentieth-Century Chicago. In R. A. Guttierez and G. Fabre (eds), *Feasts and Celebrations in North American Ethnic Communities*. Albuquerque: University of New Mexico Press.

Haas, P. (1992) Epistemic Communities and International Policy Coordination. *International Organization* 46(1), pp. 1–35.

Haddad, Y. (1983) Arab Muslims and Islamic Institutions in America: Adaptation and Reform. In S. Y. Abraham and N. Abraham (eds), *Arabs in the New World: Studies on Arab-American Communities*. Detroit: Wayne State University Press.

Haddad, Y. Y. and A. T. Lummis (1987) *Islamic Values in the United States: A Comparative Study*. New York: Oxford University Press.

Hakim, C. (1987) Trends in Flexible Workforce. *Employment Gazette* 95, pp. 549–60.

Halbwachs, M. (1992) *On Collective Memory*. Chicago: The University of Chicago Press.

Hall, S. (1997) Old and New Identities: Old and New Ethnicities. In A. D. King (ed.), *Culture, Globalization and the World System: Contemporary Conditions for the Representation of Identity*. Minneapolis: University of Minnesota Press, pp. 41–68.

Hanchard, M. (1999) Afro-Modernity: Temporality, Politics, and the African Diaspora. *Public Culture* 11(1), pp. 245–68.

Harmon, A. (1999) It's @786. Do You Know Where Your Computer Is? *New York Times*, Sunday, March 7, section 4, p. 2, Col. 5.

Harvey, D. (1989) *The Condition of Postmodernity.* Oxford: Blackwell.

Hassard, J. (1990) Preface. In *The Sociology of Time.* New York: St Martin's Press, now Palgrave Macmillan.

Held, D. *et al.* (1999) *Global Transformations: Politics, Economics and Culture.* Stanford: Stanford University Press.

Heller, D. (1999) If We Can Shop Online, We Can Vote Online. *San Francisco Chronicle.* Thursday, March 11.

Hepworth, M. (1991) Information Technology and the Global Restructuring of Capital Markets. In S. D. Brunn and T. R. Leinbach (eds), *Collapsing Space and Time.* New York: HarperCollins Academic.

Hermansen, M. K. (1994) The Muslims of San Diego. In Y. Y. Haddad and J. I. Smith (eds), *Muslim Communities in North America.* Albany: State University of New York Press.

Hinman, R. R. (1838) *The Blue Laws of New Haven Colony.* Hartford, CT: Case, Tiffany and Co.

Hogben, M. (1983) The Socio-Religious Behavior of Muslims in Canada: An Overview. In E. H. Waugh, B. Abu-Laban, and R. B. Qureshi (eds), *The Muslim Community in North America.* Edmonton: The University of Alberta Press.

Huber, H. (1958) *Geist und Buchstabe der Sonntagsruhe.* Salzburg: Otto Muller.

Husain, A. and H. Vogelaar (1994) Activities of the Immigrant Muslim Communities in Chicago. In Y. Y. Haddad and J. I. Smith (eds), *Muslim Communities in North America.* Albany: State University of New York Press.

Jacobs, L. (1995) *The Jewish Religion.* New York: Oxford University Press.

Jacobs, P. (1973) *Is Curly Jewish? A Political Self-Portrait Illuminating Three Turbulent Decades of Social Revolt 1935–1965.* New York: Vintage Books.

James, S. B. (1997) The Social Adjustment and Coping Mechanisms of Filipino Migrant Workers in Nigeria. *Asian Migrant* 10(4), pp. 104–9.

John Paul II (1998) *Dies Domini.* Apostolic Letter of the Holy Father to the Bishops, Clergy and Faithful of the Catholic Church on Keeping the Lord's Day Holy. The Vatican, May 1998, 34 pages.

Johns, W. L. (1967) *Dateline Sunday, USA: The Story of Three and a Half Centuries of Sunday-law Battles in America.* Mountain View: Pacific Press Publishing Association.

Jovanis, P. B. (1983) Telecommunication and Alternative Work Schedules: Options for Managing Transit Travel Demand. *Urban Affairs Quarterly* 2, pp. 167–89.

Kaplan, B. (1957) *The Eternal Stranger: A Study of Jewish Life in the Small Community.* New York: Bookman Associates.

Kay, J. A. and C. N. Morris (1987) The Economic Efficiency of Sunday Trading Restrictions. *Journal of Industrial Economics* 36, pp. 113–29.

Kelly, J. D. (1999) Time and the Global: Against the Homogeneous, Empty Community in Contemporary Social Theory. In B. Meyer and P. Geschiere (eds), Globalization Identity. Oxford: Blackwell, p. 268.

Kepel, G. (1987) *Les Banlieues de l'Islam. Naissance d'une Religion en France.* Paris: Editions du Seuil.

Kern, S. (1983) *The Culture of Time and Space, 1880–1918.* Cambridge, MA: Harvard University Press.

Kiesling, C. (1970) *The Future of the Christian Sunday.* New York: Sheed and Ward.

Killpert, G. B. (1980) The Sun Rises and the Sun Sets (British Case defining Day and Night). *Canadian Lawyer* 4(5), pp. 8–9.

Kilpatrick, A. (1999) Internet Time: Switch for Swatch. *Computing in Science and Engineering* 1(4), p. 5.

Kinsman, F. (1987) *The Telecommuters.* Guilford: Biddles Ltd.

Kliger, H. (ed.) (1992) *Jewish Hometown Associations and Family Circles in New York.* Bloomington: Indiana University Press.

Knox, P. and P. J. Taylor (eds) (1995) *World Cities in a World System.* New York: Cambridge University Press.

Kraft, R. A. (1965) Some Notes on Sabbath Observance in Early Christianity. *Andrews University Seminary Studies* 3, pp. 28–33.

Kristeva, J. (1981) Women's Time. *Signs* 1, pp. 16–35.

Kula, M. (1979) From Private Fatherland to Ideological Fatherland. *The Polish Sociological Bulletin* 1(45), pp. 81–7.

Kushner, J. A. (1981) Toward the Central Meaning of Religious Liberty: Non-Sunday Sabbatarians and the Sunday Closing Cases Revisited. *Southwestern Law Journal* 35(2), pp. 557–84.

Laband, D. N. and D. H. Heinbuch (1987) *Blue Laws: The History, Economics, and Politics of Sunday-Closing Laws.* Lexington, DC: Lexington Books.

Laguerre, M. S. (1999) *Minoritized Space: An Inquiry into the Spatial Order of Things.* Berkeley: University of California- Institute of Governmental Studies Press.

Laguerre, M. S. (2000) *The Global Ethnopolis: Chinatown, Japantown and Manilatown in American Society*. Basingstoke: Macmillan Press now Palgrave Macmillan.

Lahaj, M. (1994) The Islamic Center of New England. In Y. Y. Haddad and J. I. Smith (eds), *Muslim Communities in North America*. Albany: State University of New York Press.

Laidi, Z. (ed.) (1997) *Le Temps Mondial*. Paris: Editions Complexe.

Lash, S. and R. Robertson (eds) (1995) *Global Modernities*. London: Sage.

L. H. (1999) Time and Information Technology: Monochronicity, Polychronicity and Temporal Symmetry. *European Journal of Information Systems* 8(1), pp. 16–26.

Lee, H. and J. Liebenau (2000) Time and the Internet at the Turn of the Millennium. *Time and Society* 9(1), pp. 43–56.

Le Goff, L. (1980) *Time, Work and Culture in the Middle Ages*. Chicago: Chicago University Press.

Levinas, E. (1987) *Time and the Other*. Pittsburgh: Duquesne University Press.

Lewis, A. H. (1888) *Critical History of Sunday Legislation*. New York: D. Appleton and Company.

Lewis, J. D. and A. J. Weigart (1990) The Structures and Meanings of Social Time. In J. Hassard (ed.), *The Sociology of Time*. New York: St. Martin's Press, now Palgrave, 1990.

Lin, J. (1998) Globalization and the Revalorization of Ethnic Places in Immigration Gateway Cities. *Urban Affairs Review*, 34(2), pp. 313–40.

Logan, J. R. and H. L. Molotch (1987) *Urban Fortunes: The Political Economy of Place*. Berkeley: University of California Press.

Low, S. M. (1996) A Response to Castells: An Anthropology of the City. *Critique of Anthropology* 16(1), pp. 57–62.

Luhmann, N. (1982) World Time and System History. In *The Differentiation of Society*, pp. 289–324.

Lurie, W. A. (1982) *Strategies for Survival: Principles of Jewish Community Relations*. New York: KTAV Publishing House Inc.

Luther, M. The Confession of Augsburg (1530) In P. Schaff (1877) *The Creeds of Christendom*. London: Hodder.

Lynwander, L. (1991) Emergency Repair of Van on Sunday Runs Afoul of Blue Law. *The New York Times*, January 6, section 12NJ; page 2, column 1.

Marientras, R. (1985) Sur La Notion de Diaspora, in *Les Minorites a l'Age de l'Etat-Nation*. Paris: Fayard, pp. 215–26.

McCrossen, A. (2000) *Holy Day, Holiday: The American Sunday*. Ithaca: Cornell University Press.

McKinney's Consolidated Laws of New York (1988) *Annotated. Book 19. General Business Law # 1 to 351*. With Annotations From State and Federal Courts and State Agencies. St. Paul, Minn: West Publishing Co, pp. 5–30.

McKinney's Consolidated Laws of New York (1999) Annotated Book 21. General Construction Law. Brooklyn: Edward Thompson Company (Cumulative Pocket West Group).

McNiel, D. and S. S. Yu (1989) Blue Laws: Impact on Regional Retail Activity. *Population Research and Policy Review* 8, 267–8.

McRae, S. (1989) *Flexible Working Time and Family Life*. Worcester: Billing and Sons Ltd.

Mahmood, C. A. (ed.) (1998) *The Greater California American Muslims Fast Yellow Pages: Business Telephone Directory*. Fremont: Expressions-Printing/Publishing.

Maiello, F. (1996) *Histoire du Calendrier: De La Liturgie a l'Agenda*. Paris: Seuil.

Massey, D. S. and N. A. Denton (1993) *American Apartheid: Segregation and the Making of the Underclass*. Cambridge: Harvard University Press.

Markovitz, Eugene. (1969) H. P. Mendes: Architect of the Union of Orthodox Jewish Congregations of America. In *A. K. Kare* (ed.), *The Jewish Experience in America*, New York: KTAV Publishing House.

Medam, A. (1993) Diaspora/Diasporas: Archetype et Typologie. *Revue Europeenne des Migrations Internationales* 9(1), pp. 59–64.

Meijers, D. (1987) The Structural Analysis of the Jewish Calendar and its Political Implications. *Anthropos* 82(4/6), pp. 603–10.

Mercure, D. (1995) *Les Temporalites Sociales*. Paris: L'Harmattan.

Metcalf, B. (ed.) (1996) *Making Muslim Space in North America and Europe*. Berkeley: University of California Press.

Meyer, B. and P. Geschiere (1999) Globalization and Identity: Dialectics of Flow and Closure. In B. Meyer and P. Geschiere (eds), *Globalization and Identity*. Oxford: Blackwell, pp. 1–15.

Mignolo, W. D. (2000) *Local Histories/ Global Designs: Coloniality, Subaltern Knowledges, and Border Thinking*. Princeton: Princeton University Press.

Mishra, R. (1999) *Globalization and the Welfare State*. Cheltenham, UK: Edward Elgar.

Mitchell, A. (1998) Panel Schedules a Monday Release of Clinton Video. *New York Times*, Saturday September 19, vol. CXL VIII no 51, 285 p. 1 col. 6.

Modelski, G. (1994) French Thoughts on World Time. *Mershon International Studies Review*, 38, pp. 247–52.

Moore, D. D. (1975) *The Emergence of Ethnicity: New York's Jews 1920–1940*. Ph D Dissertation, Department of History, Columbia University.

Moorehouse, J. C. (1984) Is Tullock Correct About Sunday Closing Laws? *Public Choice* 42, pp. 197–203.

Moss, K. (1995) St Patrick's Day Celebrations and the Formation of Irish-American Identity, 1845–1875. *Journal of Social History* 29(1), pp. 125–48.

Moss, M. L. (1987) Telecommunications, World Cities and Urban Policy. *Urban Studies* 24, pp. 534–46.

Muhammad Ali, Maulana (ed.) (1991) *The Holy Qur'an*. Lahore, Pakistan: Ahmadiyyah Anjuman Isha'at Islam.

Naff, A. (1985) *Becoming American: The Early Arab Immigrant Experience*. Carbondale: Southern Illinois University Press.

Negroponte, N. (1995) *Being Digital*. London: Hodder and Stoughton.

Newman, M. (1999) Paterson Will Close Schools for 2 Muslim Holidays, The New York Times, May 30, 1999, section 14NJ, page 5, column 1.

Newman, S. P. (1997) *Parades and the Politics of the Street: Festive Culture in the Early American Republic*. Philadelphia: University of Pennsylvania Press.

The New York Times, October 31, 1993.

The New York Times, March 27, 1994.

The New York Times, June 16, 1995.

The New York Times, January 19, 1997.

Nguyen, D. T. (1992) The Spatialization of Metric Time: The Conquest of Land and Labor in Europe and the United States. *Time and Society* 1(1), pp. 29–50.

Nowotny, H. (1992) Time and Social Theory: Towards a Social Theory of Time. *Time and Society* 1(3), pp. 421–54.

O'Harrow Jr., R. (1994) Jewish Holiday, Opening of School Collide in Va.

The Washington Post, January 5, Section Metro, Page B1.

Olitzky, K. M. (1985) Sundays at Chicago Sinai Congregation: Paradigm for a Movement. *American Jewish History* LXXIV (3), pp. 356–68.

Osman, A.-R. A. (1999) *The Islamic Calendar 1420 A. H.* New York: The Islamic Cultural Center of New York.

Padilla, L. M. (1997) Intersectionality and Positionality. *Fordham Law Review* 66(3), pp. 843–929.

Panth, B. D. (1944) *Consider the Calendar.* New York: Teachers College.

Parry, A. (1940) The Soviet Calendar. *Journal of Calendar Reform* 10, pp. 63–9.

Pieterse, J. N. (1995) Globalization as Hybridization. In M. Featherstone *et al.* (eds), *Global Modernities*, London: Sage.

Paolucci, G. (1996) The Changing Dynamics of Working Time. *Time and Society* 5(2), pp. 145–67.

Parisot, J.-P. (1996) *Calendriers et Chronologie.* Paris: Masson.

Parisot, Jean-Paul and Francoise Suagher, (1996) *Calendriers et Chronologie.* Paris: Masson.

Price, J. and B. Yandle (1987) Labor Markets and Sunday Closing Laws. *Journal of Labor Research* 7, pp. 407–14.

Pogrebin, L. C. (1996) The High Holy Days. In J. David (ed.), *Growing Up Jewish: An Anthology.* New York: William Morrow and Company.

Porter, H. B. (1960) *The Day of Light: The Biblical and Liturgical Meaning of Sunday.* Greenwich, CT: Seabury Press.

Powell, C. L. (1995) *My American Journey.* New York: Random House.

Price, J. and B. Yandle (1987) Labor Markets and Sunday Closing Laws. *Journal of Labor Research* 7, pp. 407–14.

Pronovost, G. (1996) *Sociologie du Temps.* Bruxelles: De Boeck Universite.

Raucher, A. (1994) Sunday Business and the Decline of Sunday Closing Laws: A Historical Overview. *Journal of Church and State* 36(1), pp. 13–33.

Rakoff, Todd D. (2002) *A Time for Every Purpose: Law and the Balance of Life.* Cambridge: Harvard University Press.

Redman, B. J. (1991) Sabbatarian Accommodation in the Supreme Court. *Journal of Church and State* 33(3), pp. 495–523.

Reinhold, R. (1988) The Los Angeles Life on New York Time, *New York Times*, 3 June, Style, pp. 1–3.

Richards, E. G. (1998) *Mapping Time: The Calendar and its History.* New York: Oxford University Press.

Richardson, E. A. (1981) *Islamic Cultures in North America.* New York: The Pilgrim Press.

Riesenfeld, H. (1959) Sabbat et Jour du Seigneur, In *New Testament Essays, Studies in Memory of T. W. Manson.* Manchester: University Press.

Riesenfeld, H. (1970) *The Gospel Tradition: Essays by H. Riesenfeld.* Oxford: Oxford University Press.

Rifkin, J. (1987) *Time Wars: The Primary Conflict in Human History.* New York: Henry Holt.

Ringgold, J. T. (1891) *Sunday: Legal Aspects of the First Day of the Week.* Jersey City: Frederick D. Linn and Co.

Rippin, A. (1993) *Muslims: Their Religious Beliefs and Practices.* New York: Routledge.

Robertson, R. (1990) Mapping the Global Condition: Globalization as the Control Concept. In M. Featherstone (ed.), *Global Culture.* London: Sage.

Robertson, R. (1992) *Globalization: Social Theory and Global Culture.* London: Sage.

Robertson, R. (1995) Glocalization: Time-Space and Homogeneity-Heterogeneity. In Mike Featherstone *et al.* (eds), *Global Modernities,* London: Sage.

Rogers, M. (1998) Performing Andean Identities. *Journal of Latin American Anthropology* 3(2), pp. 2–19.

Rolland, D. (2000) *Memoire et Imaginaire de la France en Amerique Latine: La Commemoration du 14 Juillet 1939–45.* Paris: L'Harmattan.

Rordorf, W. (1968) *Sunday: The History of the day of Rest and Worship in the Earliest Centuries of the Christian Church.* Philadelphia: Westminster Press.

Rose, J. M. (1992) When is it Night in the Penal Law but not in the Criminal Procedure Law. *Law Office Economics and Management* 33(2), pp. 201–04.

Rowbotham, S. (1989) *The Past is Before Us.* London: Pandora Press.

Rudolph, S. H. (1997) Religion, States, and Transnational Civil Society. In S. H. Rudolph and J. Piscatori (eds), *Transnational Religion and Fading States,* Boulder: Westview Press, pp. 1–24.

Rudolf, S. H. and J. Piscatori (eds), *Transnational Religion and Fading States*. Boulder: Westview.

Rutz, H. J. (ed.) *The Politics of Time*. Washington DC: American Anthropological Association.

Safran, W. (1991) Diasporas in Modern Societies. *Diaspora*, 1(1), pp. 83–99.

Sanexa, S. and Mokhtarian, P. (1997) The Impact of Telecommuting on the Activity Spaces of Participants. *Geographical Analysis* 29, pp. 124–44.

Sarna, J. D. The Cult of Synthesis in American Jewish Culture. *Jewish Social Studies* 5(1–2), pp. 52–79.

Sarna, J. D. and D. G. Dalin (1997) *Religion and State in the American Jewish Experience*. Notre Dame: University of Notre Dame Press.

Sassen, S. (1998) *The Global City*. Princeton: Princeton University Press.

Schissel, M. J. (1999) Church, State, and School. *The New York Times*, section A, page 28, column 6, September 23.

Schmemann, S. (1998) Weighing Shame and Sympathy, A Weary People Watch Clinton. *The New York Times*, Tuesday September 22, vol CXL VIII, no 51, 288 p. 1.

Shackle, G. (1958) *Time in Economics*. Amsterdam: North-Holland.

Shain, Y. (1999) Marketing the American Creed Abroad: Diasporas in the US and their Homelands. New York: Cambridge University Press.

Shapiro, M. J. (2000) National Times and Other Times: Re-Thinking Citizenship. *Cultural Studies* 14(1), pp. 79–98.

Shapiro, M. and D. Neaubauer (1990) Spatiality and Policy Discourse: Reading the Global City. In R. B. J. Walker and Saul H. Mendlovitz (eds), *Contending Sovereignties: Redefining Political Community*. Boulder: Lynne Rienner Publishers, pp. 97–124.

Sheehy, G. (1995) *The Canon law: Letter and Spirit*. London: Geoffrey Chapman.

Sherman, C. B. (1961) *The Jew Within American Society: A Study in Ethnic Individuality*. Detroit: Wayne State University Press.

Simons, W. (1985) Interview with Adolph Schayes. *American Jewish History* LXXIV (3), pp. 287–307.

Smith, Jane I. (1980) *Women in Contemporary Muslim Societies*. Lewisburg: Bucknell University Press.

Smith, Jane I. (1999) *Islam in America.* New York: Columbia University Press.

Solis, D. (1985) If you Want to Make a Retailer Red-Hot, Talk About Blue Laws. *Wall Street Journal*, February 4 p. 25.

Sorin, G. (1992) *A Time for Building: The Third Migration 1880–1920.* Baltimore: Johns Hopkins University Press.

Sorokin, P. and R. Merton (1990) Social Time: A Methodological and Functional Analysis. In J. Hassard (ed.) *The Sociology of Time.* New York: St Martin's Press now Palgrave.

Smith, Joseph M. etc., *et al.* v. Community Board No. 14, *et al.* Supreme Court, Special Term, Queens County, Part 1. July 8, 1985. 491 New York Supplement 2d Series 58-1 (Sup. 1985).

Stadtmauer, M. A. (1994) Remember the Sabbath? The New York Blue Laws and the Future of the Establishment Clause. *Cardozo Arts and Entertainment Law Journal* 12(1), pp. 213–36.

Stiles, M. N. (1933) *The World's Work and the Calendar.* Boston: The Gorham Press.

Strand, K. A. (1979) *The Early Christian Sabbath.* Worthington: Ann Arbor Publishers.

Struebing, L. (1997) Internet-based Research Breaks Through Barriers of Language and Time. *Quality Progress* 30(6), p. 17.

Strum, C. (1992) On Sundays, Bergen Shoppers Rest. *The New York Times*, section B, page 6, column 4, 7 December.

Sue, R. (1994) *Temps et Ordre Social.* Paris: Presses Universitaires de France.

Sullivan, O. (1997) Time Waits for no (Wo)man: An Investigation of the Gendered Experience of Domestic Time. *Sociology* 31, pp. 221–39.

Taylor, C. (1992) *Multiculturalism and the Politics of Recognition.* Princeton: Princeton University Press.

Thomas, T. (1996) App Development in Web Time: Think of it Like Dog Years. *InfoWorld* 18(13), p. 63.

Thompson, E. (1967) Time, Work-Discipline and Industrial Capitalism. *Past and Present* 38, pp. 59–87.

Tomlinson, J. (1999) *Globalization and Culture.* Chicago: University of Chicago Press.

Trumbull, J. H. (ed.) (1876) *True-Blue Laws of Connecticut and New Haven and the False Blue Laws Invented by the Rev. Samuel Peters.* Hartford, CT: American Publishing Co.

Tullock, G. (1975) The Transitional Gains Trap. *The Bell Journal of Economics* 6, pp. 671–8.

Turner, B. S. (1991) Politics and Culture in Islamic Globalism. In R. Robertson and W. R. Garret (eds), *Religion and Global Order*, New York: Paragon House.

Vertovec, S. (1999) Conceiving and Researching Transnationalism. *Ethnic and Racial Studies* 22(2), pp. 447–62.

Vigneault, G. S. (1999) Internet Time: Why Switch for Swatch. *Computing in Science and Engineering* 1(3), p. 5.

Virilio, P. (1983) *Pure War.* New York: Semiotex(e), 1983.

Virilio, P. (1997) Positions. In Z. Laidi (ed.) *Le Temps Mondial*. Paris: Editions Complexe.

Voll, J. O. (1991) Islamic Issues for Muslims in the United States. In Y. Y. Haddad (ed.), *The Muslims in America*, New York: Oxford University Press.

Walker, G. R. and P. J. Sheppard (1999) Telepresence: The Future of Telephony. In P. J. Sheppard and G. R. Walker (eds), *Telepresence*, Boston: Kluwer Academic Publishers, pp. 1–13.

Walker, R. B. J. and Saul H. Mendlovitz (1990) *Contending Sovereignties: Redefining Political Community*. Boulder: Lynne Rienner Publishers, pp. 97–124.

Wallerstein, I. (1974) *The Modern World System 1: Capitalist Agriculture and the Origins of the European World Economy in the Sixteenth Century.* New York: Academic Press.

Wall Street Journal (1996) February 15, section B, page 6, column 4, Coke's Lunar New Year Ad.

Ward, H. H. (1960) *Space-Age Sunday.* New York: Macmillan, now Palgrave Macmillan.

Warner, S. and J. G. Wittner (eds) (1998) *Gatherings in Diasporas.* Philadelphia: Temple University Press.

Wensinck, A. J. (1954) L'influence juive sur les origines du culte musulman. *Revue Africaine* 98, pp. 85–112.

Joselit, J. W. (1990) *New York's Jewish Jews: The Orthodox Community in the Interwar Years.* Bloomington: Indiana University Press.

Westin, C. (1998) Temporal and Spatial Aspects of Multiculturality: Reflections on the Meaning of Time and Space in Relation to the Blurred Boundaries of Multicultural Societies. In R. Baubock and J. Rundell (eds), *Blurred Boundaries: Migration, Ethnicity and Citizenship*. Aldershot: Ashgate, pp. 53–84.

Wiesenberg, M. (ed.) (1963) *Official Directory of the Board of Education of the City of New York*. New York: Board of Education.

Wigoder, G. (ed.) (1989) *The Encyclopedia of Judaism*. New York: Macmillan, now Palgrave.

Willett, C. (ed.) (1998) Theorizing Multiculturalism: A Guide to the Current Debate Oxford: Blackwell.

Wilson, W. J. (1993) *The Truly Disadvantaged: The Inner City, the Underclass, and Public Policy*. Chicago: University of Chicago Press.

Wilson, G. (1988) The French Republican Calendar. In *Antiquarian Horology: The Proceedings of the Antiquarian Horological Society* 3(17).

Yaffe, J. (1968) *The American Jews*. New York: Random House.

Young, I. M. (1998) Polity and Group Difference: A Critique of the Ideal of Universal Citizenship. In G. Shafir (ed.), *The Citizenship Debates*. Minneapolis: University of Minnesota Press.

Zeitlin, S. (1930) Notes Relatives au Calendrier Juif. *Revue des Etudes Juives* 89, pp. 349–59.

Zerubavel, E. (1981) *Hidden Rhythms: Schedules and Calendars in Social Life*. Berkeley: University of California Press.

Zerubavel, E. (1982) The Standardization of Time: a Sociohistorical Perspective. *American Journal of Sociology* 88(1), pp. 1–23.

Zerubavel, E. (1985) *The Seven Day Circle: The History and Meaning of the Week*. New York: The Free Press.

Ziyadah, K. (1996) *Vendredi, Dimanche*. Arles, France: Sindbad/Actes Sud.

Index

195